Praise for
The End of Woman

"My hope is for men and women to read *The End of Woman* with a heart open to see the reality of what secular feminism has done to our society. Instead of empowering women, we are being erased. Instead of building up the strengths and abilities surrounding the unique qualities of women, we have been encouraged to deny who we were meant to be and embrace a masculine identity. This did not happen overnight. This book gives a historic look at how womanhood has been cheapened to a mere costume in our current society and serves as a warning: if we do not work now to reverse the damage that has been done, we may never be able to correct it. This is a must read."

—**Abby Johnson,** former Planned Parenthood director and current CEO of And Then There Were None

"*The End of Woman* is an insanely intelligent and vital book on why destroying womanhood and manhood hasn't made anyone happy—and never will. Through intense research and masterful writing, Carrie Gress unmasks the hideous history of feminism and invites women into an infinitely more joyful way of life."

—**Kimberly Ells,** author of *The Invincible Family: Why the Global Campaign to Crush Motherhood and Fatherhood Can't Win*

"Carrie Gress is a brilliant woman and fearless writer. Her books often strike me with a mix of shock and horror at her exposés of the rot of the culture, especially the chaos inflicted by America's cultural-sexual revolutionaries. But on the plus side, her books keep me informed and edified about the challenges facing the

nation. They are indispensable. In this latest work, Dr. Gress once again sends a warning to Americans and especially to women."

—**Paul Kengor**, professor of political science, Grove City College, and editor of the *American Spectator*

"*The End of Woman* exposes the riveting and largely unknown story behind the unfolding of the feminist movement through the lives of its pivotal figures. Gress brings to this history her philosopher's mind and a real heart for women. The result is a uniquely rich and refreshing read that connects the many dots that have led us here and the path of restoration that can guide us still."

—**Noelle Mering**, author of *Awake, Not Woke*

"Feminism's family of origin, seen in the backstories of propagandists like Wollstonecraft and Stanton, Friedan and Steinem, is carefully chronicled by Carrie Gress in her masterpiece *The End of Woman*. This cautionary tale is all we need to break with the feminist 'brand.' And to emerge from its confines, Gress suggests something both simple and radical: let women be women, particularly in our self-sacrificial love as mothers."

—**Andrea Picciotti-Bayer**, director of the Conscience Project and mother of ten

"There is so much loud noise in the culture wars. Carrie Gress's eloquent *The End of Woman* is that wonderful exception. It's a book whose tone of calm reason and argument via historical research and compassion for its subject make it go down smoothly, but without sacrificing its strong argument and core ethical values. Beautifully written and empathetic, it argues that we accept the things we cannot change about our human vulnerability while pointing the way to making sure women are respected and cared for. A first-rate work."

—**Mark Judge**, author of *The Devil's Triangle*

"Whereas second-wave feminists made popular the notion that 'the personal is political,' Carrie Gress gracefully yet unflinchingly demonstrates in *The End of Woman* that, for the women who made feminism, the political is deeply personal. We would be remiss to ignore the decadence, dysfunction, and depression that followed so many their whole lives long, and equally silly to imagine that these personal tragedies had no bearing on the ideas they very successfully memed into the reality of modern life. This excellent book is for anyone who has known the tragedy of living by lies, and who earnestly wants to see the truth, no matter how unpopular it may have become."

—**Helen Roy,** contributing editor, the American Mind

"Carrie Gress knows exactly what a woman is and what her true and marvelous purpose is. Her fascinating new book is a riveting whodunit that answers an inescapable question we are all asking ourselves: Who is responsible for murdering womanhood? Finally, we have our answer, along with an eloquent clarion call to restore women to their rightful and essential place in society."

—**Peachy Keenan,** author of *Domestic Extremist: A Practical Guide to Winning the Culture War*

THE END OF WOMAN

THE END OF WOMAN
How Smashing the Patriarchy Has Destroyed Us

CARRIE GRESS

Since 1947
REGNERY
An Imprint of Skyhorse Publishing, Inc.

Regnery books may be purchased in bulk at special discounts for sales promotion, corporate gifts, fund-raising, or educational purposes. Special editions can also be created to specifications. For details, contact the Special Sales Department, Regnery, 307 West 36th Street, 11th Floor, New York, NY 10018 or info@skyhorsepublishing.com.

Regnery® is an imprint of Skyhorse Publishing, Inc.®, a Delaware corporation.

Visit our website at www.regnery.com.
Please follow our publisher Tony Lyons on Instagram
    @tonylyonsisuncertain.

10 9 8 7 6 5 4 3 2 1

Library of Congress Cataloging-in-Publication Data is available on file.

Cover design by John Caruso
Cover photograph by Ginny Sheller

Hardcover ISBN: 978-1-68451-418-2
First paperback ISBN: 978-1-68451-529-5
eBook ISBN: 978-1-68451-435-9

Printed in the United States of America

For Ellen Louise Stark Cronkrite

&

Susan Louise Gress Andrews

who showed me how to love,
even in the face of great suffering

What you most want to find will be found
where you least want to look.

—Jordan Peterson

Contents

Vulnerability and Patriarchy

Sometime in the 1800s, a young English woman, Hester Vaughn, immigrated to the United States, lured across the Atlantic by a man who turned out to be already married. She found a job as a scullery maid and was raped by her employer. Pregnant, and forced to leave her position, she went from place to place until it was time for her child to be born. With scarcely a penny to her name, she paid for an attic room in a hotel with a broken window. There was no heat. She gave birth alone during a blizzard. Hester delivered the baby and tied a crude knot in the umbilical cord to prevent them both from bleeding to death. The baby then froze to death, its tiny body stuck to the floorboards. Hester was taken to prison and tried for infanticide.[1]

It is hard for contemporary Western women and men to wrap their minds around these dreadful kinds of stories. They come from a time when such incidents were all but commonplace. A woman was just a few fateful steps away from a life of destitution, prostitution, prison, or starvation. For many of the early feminists, these stories rightfully dredged up interior anger and courage and whetted their desire to do something, anything, to help women.

The woman's question was and still remains a question about the vulnerability of women. Although we may not see such stark examples of women's weakness in our wealthy society today, the vulnerability of being a woman has not gone away. That vulnerability is perhaps most apparent just after a woman has given birth, with her body reeling from delivery, and a helpless, tiny child needing her body, her warmth, and her tenderness to keep it alive. Motherhood makes women vulnerable. Our weakness is locked up in our fertility, our hormones, our bodily cycles, and all the functions required to give life to another. This vulnerability is what women have been struggling against since the beginning of time.

Feminists have embarked upon their own two-fold approach to mitigating this vulnerability. The first step is to help women become more like men, independent and unconstrained by nature. The second is to end the patriarchy, which has seemingly kept women in this vulnerable state from the dawn of civilization to the present era. It seems a simple enough solution, but is it working? After over a century of feminist progress and legal victories against "patriarchal oppression," do women finally "have it all"?

The Problem of Patriarchy

Smash the patriarchy! This once radical slogan is now a familiar refrain at women's marches and public protests. Most such events feature this chant, shouted with gusto, with similar slogans plastered on signs:

Read books and fight the patriarchy
It's a beautiful day to smash the patriarchy
The patriarchy isn't going to smash itself
Hex the patriarchy
Grab 'em by the patriarchy

Aside from sporting anti-patriarchy merchandise such as T-shirts and bumper stickers, women have agitated, protested, paraded, published, lobbied, and voted with determination to finally rid the world of the patriarchal menace.

Merriam-Webster defines patriarchy as "social organization marked by the supremacy of the father in the clan or family, the legal dependence of wives and children, and the reckoning of descent and inheritance in the male line" and "*broadly*: control by men of a disproportionately large share of power."[2]

Sociologist Sylvia Walby speaks more specifically, defining patriarchy as "a system of social structures and practices in which men dominate, oppress, and exploit women."[3] Feminist Kate Millett called the patriarchy "the most pervasive ideology of our culture"[4] and argued that it functioned as "a most ingenious form of 'interior colonization,'"[5] while queer theorist Judith Butler decried it as "theoretical imperialism."[6] The language of colonialism suggests that women are not only unequal, but exist as a conquered people yearning to break free from their oppressors' chains and to finally, or once again, live independently.

Central to these characterizations is the regnant belief that patriarchy is sustained by men in order to control women. Feminism, it is generally believed, developed in response to patriarchy, to finally rid the world of its injustice. Feminist Jacqueline Rose posited that "if patriarchy weren't effective, we wouldn't need feminism; if it were totally effective, we wouldn't have feminism."[7] There exists an unbreakable tension between feminism's efforts and the patriarchy's existence. Feminism fights on as an effort to restructure society by erasing the patriarchy. But what happens when the patriarchy disappears? What does the feminist endgame look like?

The attempts to overthrow and erase the patriarchy from existence have left modern women scrambling and desperate to find a place for themselves and new meaning in a hectic and anxiety-ridden modern world. The lives of historical feminists from Mary Wollstonecraft to

Shulamith Firestone present a glimpse into the motivations and roots of the world's fieriest critics of the patriarchy. Their tragic and difficult lives, especially their often-tortured relationships with men, set the course for the movement that has overthrown and reshaped our contemporary world.

What Has Happened to Women

The fight against the patriarchy began roughly with the 1792 publication of Mary Wollstonecraft's book *A Vindication of the Rights of Woman*, with its call for radically restructuring society, erasing male hierarchies, and ushering in a more egalitarian vision of the sexes. It has been gaining steam ever since, through the suffrage movement, the post-suffrage era, the arrival of communism, and up through the radical feminism of the 1960s and '70s. Through all these years of picketing, marching, and leaning in, there seem to be some largely overlooked problems that have simultaneously arisen for women with the destruction of the patriarchy. Here are several of the most evident.

The first: Our society can no longer define "woman." In a documentary of that title, Matt Walsh demanded an answer to the question "What is a woman?" He posed this question to men and women far and wide, and, at least in the West, the question was generally met with a blank stare, a grasping for language, or an awkward laugh. No one offered a definition. The only real answer Walsh gets, in the end, is from his wife. A woman is an adult female human.[8] Simple enough. Of course, there is more to it, but this is a starting point.

One might think that, with all this emphasis on feminism, women would have some sort of answer as to what women are—an answer that could easily distinguish women from men in our achievements and aspirations, and that would provide a clear understanding of what our gifts are and why we are proud to be women. As of now, we cannot do any of this.

Perhaps the highest profile case of not being able to define woman-hood was Judge Ketanji Brown Jackson's 2022 confirmation hearing for the Supreme Court. Rather than answering the question of what a woman is, she declared that she couldn't define womanhood without a biology degree.[9]

The second issue is that men are now edging women out of prized positions and awards while wearing dresses and heels. The hottest flash-point in the culture today is the transgender movement, with the progressive mob even coming after feminists, such as the famed author of the Harry Potter series, J. K. Rowling. Anyone who dares to oppose the idea that men can become women (or vice versa) is targeted. Activists use the derogatory term "trans-exclusionary radical feminists," or "TERFs," to criticize those who, like Rowling, embrace the idea that a woman is someone who is a biological female, from birth, distinct from mere gender expression.

Meanwhile, biological men in women's clothing have increasingly encroached on celebrity, sports, and politics. *TIME* magazine's "Woman of the Year" Caitlyn Jenner, the first "female" four-star admiral in the Commissioned Corps Rachel Levine and the NCAA "female" swimming champion Lia Thomas are all lauded as examples of female achievement, despite their radically distinct hormonal base-lines, higher testosterone levels, and greater physical strength, especially in the upper body.

To accommodate these new "women," the *Cambridge Dictionary* released a new definition of womanhood in 2022, including those who identify as trans women; it reads, "an adult who lives and identifies as female though they may have been said to have a different sex at birth."[10] *Merriam-Webster* also amended its definition of woman to include those "having a gender identity that is the opposite of male."[11]

On top of everything else, women are not happy. A dramatic 2009 study issued by the National Bureau of Economic Research revealed that women are not growing happier as feminist ideals are embraced.[12] In fact, the opposite is true. In the 1970s, women rated their overall life satisfaction higher than men did, but it has been on the steady decline ever since. The study revealed that "women of all education groups have become less happy over time with declines in happiness having been steepest among those with some college."[13] The study also concluded that "on average, women are less happy with their marriage than men and women have become less happy with their marriage over time."[14] This data helps to explain why nearly 70 percent of divorces are initiated by women.[15]

General happiness metrics confirm that women are struggling under the current conditions and are seeking medical attention as a result. Suicide, depression, substance abuse, and sexually transmitted infections have all increased dramatically over the last five decades. Women are not becoming happier, just more medicated.

Much of women's unhappiness can also be tied to the rise of "bureaugamy." Bureaugamy is a term coined by the sociologist Lionel Tiger, who also coined "male bonding," and refers to the new relationship that women with children have with the state. In the past, the economic needs of a mother were met primarily by a husband who had a vested interest in providing for the growth and well-being of his family and who helped shoulder shared responsibilities within the family. But as more and more women have children out of wedlock, there is ever greater pressure on the state to fill the void. Bureaugamy is the relationship that has developed in which a woman's core needs are met by the state, and not her father or spouse.[16] The progressive solution has been to fix or shore up problems with the help of more government assistance and programs to take the place the family once held. The Obama administration developed Julia, an imaginary woman who never needed a man but had her cradle-to-grave needs supplied by the government, as a political model to shore up any vulnerability that women experience.[17] The model makes responsible, loving, and virtuous men obsolete.

Feminism has pitted the sexes against each other. Rather than looking, as men and women, for solutions to their problems together, both sides continue to hurl blame across the aisle in an endless argument. Women blame men, and men blame women. The rift is felt everywhere but is rarely healed, as politics and rhetoric elide personal relationships.

Feminism's Faults

It is time for honest women to recognize that feminism has not been the boon for women that it has been presented as. To be sure, there have been many advances under feminism, such as laws against sex and pregnancy discrimination, custody laws for mothers, and many social and economic opportunities. But to focus on these genuine improvements is to overlook the irreparable harm feminism has done to legions of women. Women were told that abortion is consequence-free, that hookup culture and casual sex are normal, and that hormonal therapies (for birth control or as puberty blockers) have no side effects. What is becoming clearer with each passing generation is that free love and consequence-free sex have come at a cost, and most of that cost is borne by those who can least afford it—poor women who will never find husbands, women and girls caught up in human trafficking or the trans craze, and children who will never know their fathers. Feminism has likewise been awful for men, but it has been particularly awful for children, especially children of unmarried parents.

It is time to look behind the curtain.

This book is a rare examination of the historical ideologies that have driven and shaped feminism. What has resulted did not happen overnight but is part of a much larger project that goes back even to the 1700s. It is a little-known story, with elements closely concealed for fear that the truth might become widely known. And it is certainly a story that has yet to be finished. Truly, there were (and remain) injustices to women that needed rectifying—for example, today homicide is among the top causes of maternal death in the United States.[18] This book is not arguing that we as a society should go back to the 1780s, or the 1880s, or even the 1950s. I remain grateful for the opportunities that I have as a woman. But it is also possible to lament the way those opportunities came about. Instead of inspiring women to flourish as women and recognizing women's vulnerability, the goal has been to make women act, hope, and dream like men, impervious to perceived weaknesses associated with womanhood. Our freedoms have come at a terrible cost, frequently at the expense of others—particularly the very, very small: the unborn. It would have been possible to achieve what we have as women without erasing womanhood altogether.

When I first started researching this book, I wasn't quite sure what I would find. I expected to find some nice platitudes about women, about the right to vote and the need for better education. I didn't start writing this book with the intention of debunking feminism from its earliest stages. Like many others—having looked carefully at the radical ideas of feminism's second wave—I thought feminism had been coopted at some point.

I could scarcely have imagined what I unearthed.

The seeds of present feminist ideas were sown even in the movement's earliest stages. Over the years, some have speculated that there was a major break in feminism from the early suffrage days, between the first wave of the suffragettes and the second wave that arrived in the 1960s. A closer look reveals that feminism wasn't hijacked by the second wave, making it into something new. Rather, several founding ideas generated from socialist, egalitarian, and secular concepts in the late 1700s developed over time. These ideas broadened and grew from small seeds as feminism went from a fringe movement to the monolithic belief system accepted by a majority of Western women today.

Feminists have continued along unchallenged, in part because most women are not well versed in feminist thought. Instead, most rely on the opinions and influence of others to form opinions about what feminism really is. In her book *Bad Feminist*, Roxane Gay speaks for many such women:

> I openly embrace the label of bad feminist. I do so because I'm flawed and human. I am not terribly well versed in feminist history. I am not as well read in key feminist texts as I would like to be. I have certain…interests and personality traits and opinions that may not fall in line with mainstream feminism, but I am still a feminist.[19]

Most of us don't know much about where feminist ideas come from but, like Gay, we still embrace the basic tenets of feminism and the ideal of equality for women. Too often, however, women heap guilt on other women who question the movement. Gay explains this sentiment: "I get angry when women disavow feminism and shun the feminist label but say they support all the advances born of feminism because I see a disconnect that does not need to be there."[20] But there are real problems at the core of feminism, most of which are unknown. Unlike any other "ism" in the world today, feminism is one we aren't supposed to question. We are meant to embrace it with our whole hearts, because to do otherwise would be to betray ourselves as women, or so the argument goes. As a result, most women view feminism as something for which they should be grateful, like a beneficent grandmother who has patiently watched over them and guided them to a happier and more just world.

This book considers the history behind feminism's founding, pro-liferation, and dissemination and questions what isn't supposed to be questioned. It will examine how we arrived at a point in history at which a significant portion of the population considers feminism the default position. Few can imagine anything else.

Feminism's failure, at root, is its misdiagnosis of what ails women. Feminists have worked hard to mitigate women's suffering, but by trying to eliminate our vulnerability, by making us cheap imitations of men, and by ignoring our womanhood. Setting off in the wrong direction, the prescribed fix can't really fix anything. Instead, it has erased women one slow step at a time. As those slow steps get faster and faster, women find themselves at risk of being erased from the movement that once purported to liberate them, finding themselves undefined in an increasingly progressive world.

Who Is This Book For?

This is a book for all women, of any background, but especially for those who are struggling and feel frustrated that the future they were promised hasn't materialized in their lives. It is for the women who have told me, "I know something isn't quite right, but I can't put my finger on the problem." And it is for women who want to be women instead of whatever the culture is telling us to be.

This is also a book for men who are tired and frustrated with the double standards that attack men's vices, while heralding those of women; for men who love their wives and daughters, sisters and mothers—but have a hard time watching the women they love destroy their lives—or men who can't figure out how to love them well; and for men who are just ready to give up on women entirely.

Jordan Peterson, in a conversation with Camille Paglia, affirmed that it must be women, not men, who finally bring down the feminist ideology. Paglia, on the other hand, suggested that men need to stand up to feminists. Peterson says that his wife has also suggested this, but this suggestion has a glaring problem. As a man, he explained, there aren't any socially acceptable ways for him to assert himself when in conflict with women. He adds:

> I know how to stand up to a man, who's...unfairly trespassing against me. And the reason I know that is because the parameters for my resistance are quite well defined, which is we talk, we argue, we push, and then it becomes physical....If we move beyond the boundaries of civil discourse, we know what the next step is. Okay? That's forbidden in discourse with women.[21]

Peterson makes a great point about the limits upon physical fighting that men should understand when it comes to conflict with women. Men hate to fight with, or even just disagree with, women because the rules of engagement are not clear. Peterson wasn't counting on the satirical Socrates of Matt Walsh, who came to women's rescue using a totally different skill set. Walsh, armed only with one of the most basic questions known to man, simply asks, "What is a woman?" With this question, he has done more for real women than most any woman has in the last fifty years. Feminism has left a trail of tears, misery, and confusion. Walsh demonstrates that we need the attention, thought, work, and love of both men and women to finally slay this ideological dragon.

Some of the details in this book might sound unbelievable. You might find yourself asking, "Why haven't I heard about this before?" This is a question I have asked myself. Why hasn't someone already written this book?

The short answer is that there are many people who couldn't write this book. If a man did, his efforts would be tossed aside as "the patriarchy." It also had to be written by a woman who didn't have to fear that the deep entrenchment of feminism would destroy her academic or journalistic career—I have neither. The longer answer, however, will become clearer as the chapters unfold and we sift through history, piecing together the threads of this baffling story.

Whenever possible, I've used resources written by those who embrace feminism instead of books written by feminism's critics. Perhaps in the style of Chaya Raichik of Libs of TikTok, which reposts the actual videos of the progressive left, more often than not I'm merely holding up what was actually said, done, or believed throughout more than two centuries of feminist thought and activism.

This book is divided into four parts. Part I explores the early development of feminism into its contemporary iteration, following the lives of many well-known feminists and their various contributions to the movement; part II moves to the way feminism became the identifying narrative of Western women; and part III explains how the women's movement led directly to the gay rights, and now trans, movements. Part IV identifies the broader ramifications of feminism's rise, and the negative effects upon civilization, ending with a close look at womanhood and ignoring the taboo on defining what a woman is.

This book examines several philosophical threads that comprise many of the ideologies discussed here, following them through more than two hundred years of use and development. Many of these ideas can feel daunting, but it might help to remember that these ideas play a role much like the role that brands play in our lives today, such as Nike, Apple, and Amazon. Like international companies, few philosophers think of ideas out of the blue. In the same way that brands borrow concepts, colors, markets, messaging, and material trends, philosophers engage with idea trends of other philosophers. As with brands, the philosopher is either copying someone, tweaking an idea, adding to it in a new way, or reacting against it. We recognize these types of patterns in brands with fads and knockoffs, but most of us don't realize how recycled and trendy philosophical ideas are. An ideology often starts with the idea of one philosopher that becomes like a brand. The more popular the ideology, the better a job its adherents have done "marketing" it and updating it each season so it stays fresh. Feminism has been a very successful ideological quasi-brand with remarkable staying power. Brands are focused mainly on monetary wealth in sales and revenues; an ideology's currency is power. Feminism, perhaps second only to Marxism, is currently the most powerful brand in the world.

PART I

The Lost Girls

These first five chapters will look at the development of feminism from a nascent idea, in the first wave, to the radical and groundbreaking theories in Betty Friedan's *The Feminine Mystique* that started the second wave. Among nearly every woman involved in feminist thought, from Wollstonecraft and the early suffrage movement to Simone de Beauvoir, Betty Friedan, Kate Millett, Shulamith Firestone, Gloria Steinem, and Phyllis Chesler, the common thread is that all of these women were broken—broken either by parental abuse, sexual trauma, drug use and abuse, or mental illness.[1] Some of these women experienced all of these wounds. Many of these women were surrounded by a remarkable number of awful men, whom we will meet in these pages: Percy Bysshe Shelley, Lord Byron, Cornelius Vanderbilt, Henry Ward Beecher, Jean-Paul Sartre, and Hugh Hefner. It isn't difficult to find the motivation for their thought.

Looking at these women's lives, a pronounced pattern emerges. The pattern is at first difficult to discern, because it is usually found behind a maelstrom of suffering, men behaving badly, and the difficult job of parsing out what is justice and what goes beyond justice.

Their now predictable reaction to their circumstances was the belief that "the system" must be thrown out and that women must become free from the demands of men, children, and family life. Most moved away from convention, seeing it as the source of their problems, and moved toward free love and self-actualization, unencumbered by men, children, or the home.

These lost girls are the women who have shaped the way most modern women, and men, think and have formed the basis of our current gendered politics and cultural norms.

CHAPTER 1

Mary, the First Feminist

Meghan Markle, Duchess of Sussex, might not appear to have much in common with an eighteenth-century common Englishwoman, but it wouldn't be a stretch to say that, intellectually, she is indebted to the first feminist, Mary Wollstonecraft (1759–1797).

The American actress and divorcée married into the twelve-hundred-year-old British monarchy when she wed Prince Harry in 2018. She quickly found the traditions, customs, and duties stifling and confining. In a much-publicized break, the duke and duchess left their work as royals, moving their growing family to Southern California. At different stages, Meghan spoke out against the royal family and then appeared on an Oprah Winfrey special where she spoke of the difficulty of royal life and the alleged racism of one unnamed family member.

In the break with the family, the duchess has not been silent about her disdain for the hierarchy or the patriarchy, in a way similar to Mary Wollstonecraft centuries ago. Meghan's exit—"Megxit"—from the hierarchy (or "The Firm") is a clear signal that Meghan remains committed to tearing down the patriarchy—and by extension any hierarchy—no matter what the cost.[1] Prince Harry, who also considers himself a feminist, calls the term Megxit misogynistic, presumably because it uses her name and not his.[2] As a descriptor, however, Megxit reflects the effort by a woman to create her own life, outside of any of the demands of family, society, or social convention. As we will see, this is another very Wollstonecraft-y idea.

Markle, perhaps one of the most privileged and entitled women in all of history, is now producing a podcast, *Archetypes*, that features her and her friends talking about women's oppression. "She's flinging open the proverbial doors to her life," gushed a reporter for The Cut. "As any millennial woman whose feminism was forged in the girlboss era would understand, she has taken a hardship and turned it into content."[3]

Meghan's hardship, of course, is something that is hotly debatable given that it was largely self-inflicted. But her privilege cannot be denied. Read this description of her home in Montecito, California: "The Montecito house is the kind of big that startles you into remembering that unimaginable wealth is actually someone's daily reality. It evokes a classic Tuscan villa, a Napa vineyard, and a manicured Beverly Hills country club decorated with careful, considered coastal tones for a casual air—the home equivalent of billionaires dressing down in denim."[4] Meghan's privilege, which came from marrying into one of the last remaining monarchies, has provided her with significant influence, wealth, and celebrity status. Ironically, it is precisely through her connection to the monarchy, one of the oldest hierarchies known to man, that she has the capacity to tear down the hierarchy she married into. She married into power and privilege only to undermine power and privilege.

While there seems to be nothing similar in the lives of Markle and Mary Wollstonecraft materially or biographically beyond their disdain for hierarchy, the fingerprints of Wollstonecraft's ideas have been imprinted on the duchess's thought. Wollstonecraft's work and that of her family, which we will explore in the next chapter, served as a type of small Russian nesting doll that had all the characteristics that would define the feminist movement already painted upon it. All that needed to happen was for it to be replicated in bigger and more dramatic ways. To explain, our story needs to go back to the days of the world's first feminist.

The feminist story begins with the French Revolution. Like most revolutions, it began with purportedly noble objectives, but something came dramatically unhinged after Madame Guillotine started lopping off the heads of the republic's enemies. Seventeen thousand would lose their heads in the Reign of Terror, justified by the effort to form a new French Republic dedicated to liberty, equality, and brotherhood, while another ten thousand died in prison, never tried for their alleged crimes.

Maximilien Robespierre and his henchmen required all good republicans to take an oath of fidelity to the state, but it was an oath that French Christians, particularly priests and nuns, couldn't take, because it put the state in God's place. The punishment for such infidelity was death.

The city of Nantes decided to deliver death to the enemies of the republic in its own preferred way. Hundreds of priests who would not take the oath of fidelity were rounded up and drowned in the local river in what were called "republican baptisms." The revolutionaries did not stop there but continued with priests and nuns, disrobing them, tying them up in couples, and then drowning them together in what were called "republican weddings."

Finally, eleven cloistered nuns were taken to the scaffold. These women, dubbed the Martyrs of Compiègne, offered themselves as martyrs for the sake of France. Ten days later, Robespierre and his Reign of Terror would come to an end, also by the guillotine.

Cleaving Culture

The French Revolution represented a dramatic shift in culture, even more so than the American Revolution. America's revolution was against British rule for the sake of freedom, but the French Revolution was an effort to recreate and reshape society in a world without God. It was an effort to erase the sacred from society and to hoist man and the state as the solution to all of humanity's problems. Reason had become the new beacon of wisdom and light. Practically speaking, the science and reason of the citizens were to be the avenues for the future, ushering in an era of liberty, equality, and brotherhood.

"In one word," Robespierre explained, "we want to fulfill the wishes of nature, accomplish the destiny of humanity, keep the promises of philosophy, absolve Providence from the long reign of crime and tyranny."[5] What emerged from the social rubble of the French Revolution were new fault lines of conflict, where the older questions informed by sacred ideals were attacked and replaced under a new desacralized order.

The French Revolution was the first major break with the sacred order around which Western society and culture had been arranged for centuries in the Judeo-Christian tradition. The sacred, such as doctrines of the Church or the Ten Commandments, no longer had a public place with the establishment of the secular order. The voice of the Catholic Church in particular, was shut away into a place of great silence, literally and culturally. According to the revolutionaries, there would now be a "new church," the church of reason, the church made by man, decorated with every great thought. God was finally to be excised from the fabric of society. Morality, then, needed a new mooring, and for many that was reason. The revolutionaries along with thinkers like Rousseau suggested that virtue was the true route to a strong republic, but it wasn't the Christian virtues of faith, hope, love, and prudence;

rather this was an attempt to reclaim an anemic ancient idea of virtue built on the notion that the human mind, when acting in accord with reason, is virtuous.[6] Patience, courage, or perseverance, and so on were not the virtues the enlightened thinkers had in mind. Virtue, or the exercise of reason, would replace the hole left by faith. However, what they didn't realize was that reason too left moral ideals wide open to the changes of moods, fashions, and fads, a pattern we will see more of in future chapters.

This era was punctuated by eradicating taboos, like monogamous marriage, and was exemplified by Marquis de Sade (1740–1814), who would become the father of what is now known as sadism. A spoiled and decadent boy, de Sade grew up to be a cruel, vile, blasphemous member of the aristocracy. De Sade spent most of his adult life in prison for his vicious and torturous crimes, using those thirty-six years to write stories and political philosophy describing his desire to live in extreme freedom without laws, religion, or morality. His life and his works take reason and liberty to their most extreme end, unencumbering man from any social constraint. His echo is heard today in the sadism of books such as E. L. James's *Fifty Shades of Grey.*

Certainly, all was not perfect under the old sacred order, with corrupt churchmen, like the Abbé de Sade (a member of the French clergy), the Marquis de Sade's uncle, who introduced his young nephew to the world of debauchery. Such scandals fueled public outrage against what was supposed to be a sacred order. But the new order—which promised to bring in peace, unity, and brotherhood—would elicit the opposite of those ideals in a magnitude never before seen, as evidenced by the bloodshed of the twentieth century. The Reign of Terror was but a foretaste of the death, horror, and utter viciousness that would engulf the globe in the centuries ahead.

This was the backdrop for the world's first feminist.

Mother of Feminism

Mary Wollstonecraft has long been considered the mother of feminism, writing colorfully about reshaping society by ridding it of the male hierarchy, what she called "the tyranny of men." Her thought, however, did not appear in a vacuum. It was influenced significantly by the Enlightenment thinkers around her and the intellectual thrust of the French Revolution.

Wollstonecraft was born into a poor Irish family on April 27, 1759, the second of the seven children of Edward and Elizabeth Wollstonecraft. The family moved frequently around Ireland and England, fleeing creditors to build a new life elsewhere.

Her father, an alcoholic, was just as likely to be joyful as vicious. His moods were unpredictable, and when in a volatile mood, he showed little restraint in whom he terrorized. Wollstonecraft recalled that one day he hanged the family dog in a fit of rage. Her father was also known for brutally raping and beating his wife. A biography described the situation:

> [Elizabeth Wollstonecraft's] terrible wordless outcries swept
> through the thin walls of their house straight into Mary's
> room, where she lay chafing against her mother's helpless-
> ness as well as her own. Finally, when she was a teenager, she
> rebelled, setting up camp outside her mother's door, waiting for
> her father to come home so she could stop him from crossing
> the threshold. But her efforts to save Elizabeth only made mat-
> ters worse. Edward pushed her out of the way and Elizabeth
> accused Mary of inflaming her father's rage, but Mary did not
> stop trying. Night after night, she took up her post.[7]

Mary's mother was described as "the first and most submissive of [Edward's] subjects."[8] Mary resented her father for his abuse and her mother for tolerating it. Her life was punctuated by crass cruelty, continual waves of poverty, and precious little capacity to change any of it.

Mary's conflict with her parents didn't end with her father's abuse. Her mother was not shy about which of her children she loved the most: her eldest son, Ned. Elizabeth showered little affection or gratitude on the others, including Mary, who quickly became a surrogate mother for her younger siblings. Even on her deathbed, Mary, who yearned for maternal affection and affirmation, heard Elizabeth's last words. They were not the apology Mary had hoped for after years of abuse and neglect, but rather, "A little patience and all will be over."[9] Perhaps it was these few words of resignation and perceived defeat that led Mary to say so much in her adult life.

As a girl, Mary was shown great kindness by a neighbor and clergyman, Mr. Clare, who had an extensive library where she was able to soak up the wisdom and folly of the ages. A loquacious girl, she absorbed much. She also formed a friendship with an accomplished young woman, Frances Blood (Fanny) who influenced Mary's young and lively mind.

In 1778, determined to leave her discordant home, Mary went to work in Bath for two years to care for a challenging elderly woman, Mrs. Dawson, until her own mother's health began to wane. She came home to care for Elizabeth until she died, and after that, Mary left her paternal home for the last time in 1783. She moved in with Fanny's family, the Bloods, while she, two of her sisters, and Fanny opened a school. Fanny died in 1785, leaving Wollstonecraft devastated. She was forced to close the school. After two years as a governess, she decided to try supporting herself as an author, creating a new "genus" for working women.

Wollstonecraft befriended radical publisher Joseph Johnson in London, who offered to publish her writings. Her first book was about raising daughters, followed by several others, along with many articles published in Johnson's literary magazine, the *Analytical Review*. Mary was made famous by her 1790 book, *A Vindication of the Rights of Men*, which was well received in both England and France. She flourished in this intellectual environment and met many like-minded intellectuals, including Thomas Paine and William Godwin, both of whom would make distinct impressions on her life.

Her most famous book, *A Vindication of the Rights of Woman* (1792), which will be discussed below, was dedicated to French statesman Charles-Maurice de Talleyrand-Périgord, the former bishop laicized by Pope Pius VII for his commitment to free love and support of the French Revolution. Mary offered it with the great hope that her ideas about equal education for boys and girls would make their way into the fabric of the new French Republic. Talleyrand later paid her a visit in London after having read her work, signaling his approval of her efforts.

With the French Revolution well underway, Mary was particularly interested in French politics and its ramifications for women, should a republic built on virtue (reason) succeed. In 1793, Mary made her way to France with the great expectation of watching the revolution unfold firsthand. She saw it as a "glorious *chance*...of attaining more virtue and happiness than has hitherto blessed our globe."[10]

Mary's life changed dramatically when she met the American importer Gilbert Imlay while in Paris. The relationship between them developed quickly, with a child soon on the way. They did not marry, but Imlay told the United States embassy that they had married, so that Mary would have protection as an American citizen from any republican reprisals as the French Revolution grew hotter and bloodier. During this time, as the Reign of Terror intensified, many of Mary's friends were imprisoned or guillotined. Shortly after the birth of their child, Fanny, Imlay abandoned Mary, leaving her a single mother. She made strenuous efforts to repair the relationship while he took on new lovers and flitted in and out of Mary's life. In 1795, Wollstonecraft returned to England, much worse for wear, and deeply traumatized by the atrocities of the Terror. Her relationship with Imlay was, to her, still an open question because of Imlay's inconsistent behavior. Despairing over him and the unraveling of their relationship, Mary attempted suicide twice. Eventually, all strings were cut between the two, although Mary continued to call herself Mrs. Imlay.

In 1796, Mary moved on to a new relationship. She had met William Godwin in 1791, a meeting arranged by her publisher along with Thomas Paine, the American known for writing *Common Sense*, a defense of the American Revolution. Years later, Godwin recollected this meeting with Wollstonecraft and Paine: "I...heard her, very frequently when I wished to hear Paine."[11] Mary dominated the entire conversation as Paine quietly ate his meal, and Godwin seethed at not getting to hear more from Paine.

But after they met again, Godwin decided that he wasn't so perturbed by Mary's chatter. They were a few years older, wiser, and mellowed through suffering, and a relationship grew between them. In short order, Mary was pregnant again. They decided to marry, a remarkable concession for both, but particularly for Godwin. He had secured a reputation as a declared anarchist, and had described "possession of a woman" in marriage as "odious selfishness."[12] He believed that the family was the enemy of happiness because of its "unnatural" enslavement of male sexuality. Wollstonecraft agreed with Godwin on this point, but she saw difficulties, particularly the harsh judgment of society for children born out of wedlock, having experienced it with her first daughter Fanny. Already her pioneering spirit was in conflict with her maternal instincts and the usefulness of certain conventions. The tightrope between radicalism and motherhood will be a consistent inflection point in feminist thinkers.

The Godwins developed an extraordinary living situation for their time, with rooms rented several doors away from their main residence so that each could have his or her own place to work. Efforts were made for Mary to have time to work on her own writing each day, instead of only taking care of the household and little Fanny. Godwin was supposed to help domestically but was wholly unsuited for the task. Even in bowing to the convention of marriage, they created a working marriage that suited their unique situation.

Mary and William were married on March 29, 1797, at Saint Pancras Church, and their daughter was born in September. Tragically, Mary passed away ten days later from an infection. Her influence has extended well beyond her own lifespan, with *A Vindication of the Rights of Woman* in particular. Godwin later published Mary's biography, detailing her romantic relationships, her pregnancies, and her suicide attempts. This significantly narrowed the public's interest in her. The public was unmoved by the message of virtue and chastity when it came from a woman who didn't appear to live by either.

The Book

Wollstonecraft's best-known work, *A Vindication of the Rights of Woman*, was truly where she cut new feminist cloth. Wollstonecraft was a contemporary of Jane Austen, and her prose, which can sound like endless chatter, would have fit easily into an Austen novel. One can almost hear Elinor Dashwood in *Sense and Sensibility* say of her, "I do not think she drew breath from the moment we left London." William Godwin had thought the same of her upon their first meeting.[13] Mary Wollstonecraft was but the first in a long line of feminists who wrote in difficult and inaccessible prose.[14] Her book's rambling and erratic structure makes it difficult to read her work and tease out her exact meaning. Aside from those challenges, many themes in *A Vindication of the Rights of Woman* made it a groundbreaking composition, earning Wollstonecraft the posthumous title of the world's first feminist—although that particular term would come much later. For our purposes, she offers three main points of interest: first, that society must be fundamentally restructured away from male hierarchy; second, that women's education must change; and third, that females need to be reclassified to ensure that their dignity is respected.

Restructuring Society

At the beginning of *A Vindication of the Rights of Woman*, Mary rails again the monarchy, which is unsurprising given the political climate, but she doesn't stop there, going on to attack the military and the Church as male institutions. Mary describes her view of the army and the Church as follows:

> A standing army, for instance, is incompatible with freedom; because subordination and rigour are the very sinews of military discipline; and despotism is necessary to give vigour to enterprizes that one will directs. A spirit inspired by romantic notions of honour, a kind of morality founded on the fashion of the age, can only be felt by a few officers, whilst the main body must be moved by command, like the waves of the sea; for the strong wind of authority pushes the crowd of subalterns forward, they scarcely know or care why, with headlong fury.[15]

Here she is emphasizing that it is just those at the top who receive the benefits of the army, while the rest are like drones acting in accord with the leaders' will. She continues:

> May I be allowed to extend the comparison to a profession where more mind is certainly to be found; for the clergy have superior opportunities of improvement, tho' subordination

almost equally cramps their faculties? The blind submission imposed at college to forms of belief serves as a novitiate to the curate, who must obsequiously respect the opinion of his rector or patron, if he means to rise in his profession. Perhaps there cannot be a more forcible contrast than between the servile dependent gait of a poor curate and the courtly mien of a bishop. And the respect and contempt they inspire render the discharge of their separate functions equally useless.[16]

Wollstonecraft was a strong critic of rote memorization in school and truly wanted children—boys and girls—to think for themselves. She appears to be taking this criticism and applying it to the Church and the unique but serious function of obedience within its own hierarchy. The curate, in her view, is useless because he has no mind of his own, and the bishop is equally useless because he is puffed up with pride because his directives of any nature or whim are followed mindlessly.

Wollstonecraft targets these masculine institutions because they are built on obedience and what she considers childish rituals. It is these institutions, she believes, that maintain society's status quo, giving power to men and perpetuating the oppression of women. Like the hierarchies she describes, men resemble the pompous bishop while women are expected to be the mindless curates. "But not content with this natural pre-eminence [their biological strength], men endeavour to sink us still lower, merely to render us alluring objects for a moment."[17] For these reasons, Mary wanted hierarchies to be erased, with society redrawn without their presence and what she believed to be the consequent oppression of women.

Equality

Wollstonecraft's main goal, like that of the architects of the French Revolution, was equality. The egalitarian movement was growing stronger, particularly in the work of her friend Thomas Paine, who had been an ardent encourager of her work since they met in 1791. He tried, however, to keep his involvement in "the women's question" out of the public eye so that it wouldn't distract from his other political commitments.[18]

Women's education, for Wollstonecraft, was the best way to restructure society to bring about equality. Both men and women—especially upper class women—receive her harsh critique in what she saw as girls' miseducation. She argued that both sexes share the blame for the state women are in, albeit unequal shares. Wollstonecraft rails against upper class women specifically for their pandering and coquettishness, their attachment to clothing and vanity, and their lack of reason. All these, she argues, are a grave disservice to women. But she also places plenty of blame on men. She writes:

> One cause of this barren blooming I attribute to a false system of education, gathered from the books written on this subject by men who, considering females rather as women than human creatures, have been more anxious to make them alluring mistresses than rational wives; and the understanding of the sex has been so bubbled by this specious homage, that the civilized women of the present century, with a few exceptions, are only anxious to inspire love, when they ought to cherish a nobler ambition, and by their abilities and virtues exact respect.[19]

Certainly, the books men wrote are part of the problem, but the bigger issue for Wollstonecraft is that men have developed a systemic way to keep women as delightful playthings, uneducated, and sexually available. The way to overcome this subjugation is virtue. While admitting bodily differences, Wollstonecraft did not believe there were differences in virtues between the sexes. Like Rousseau and others, she uses virtue to mean the exercise of reason. "In fact," she writes, "it is a farce to call any being virtuous whose virtues do not result from the exercise of its own reason."[20] Virtue had an added benefit beyond just underpinning a moral character: it was supposed to create good citizens. Virtuous people made good citizens. Additionally, if one appeared to be a good citizen but harbored "superstition" or put one's Christian faith higher than the state, that made one both immoral and a bad citizen. If a sufficient number of citizens were virtuous, Wollstonecraft made plain, then the republic would thrive; but it would fail if too many were vicious.[21] And "the more equality there is established among men," she explained, "the more virtue and happiness will reign in society."[22] Equality, as sameness, and virtue were Mary's main goal for all men, and women needed to be educated appropriately to make this vision a reality.

Although Wollstonecraft was horrified by the tyrannical nature of Robespierre in the French Revolution, the two had a similar understanding of the role of virtue in this new enlightened era. It is through this lens that one can understand how Robespierre was able to combine virtue and terror in this statement:

> If virtue be the spring of a popular government in times of peace, the spring of that government during a revolution is virtue combined with terror: virtue, without which terror is destructive; terror, without which virtue is impotent. Terror is only justice prompt, severe and inflexible; it is then an emanation of virtue.[23]

These are the republican virtues that would lead to good citizens, not to saints.[24] This is why Wollstonecraft's work resonated with Talleyrand, who was interested in forming ideal citizens for his new republic of reason, and he believed that such virtue could only be inculcated by good public education.

While it is laudable that Wollstonecraft wanted to increase virtue in women, the problem was what she meant by virtue and its attachment to reason that focused on being a citizen, apart from any kind of hierarchy. The state becomes the guiding light, but as the French Revolution demonstrated, the state can have its own vicious principles untethered from reason. These ideas are rather commonplace to us today, but they help to contextualize early socialist stirrings that we will see bloom later with the communist revolutions.

Woman as Human Being

The final important idea in Wollstonecraft's work is her emphasis on the female as a human creature or rational creature and not as a woman, which builds on her idea of natural and rational equality. This thread will be one we see tugged on repeatedly throughout the coming chapters as feminism moves forward. The emphasis is on a notion of a female as a human being, apart from being a woman or mother. The capacity for motherhood, in this view, is somehow not essential to being a female human. The idea rests on the belief that having and raising children is what is keeping female humans from being "real" people. This is one of the ideas that will open the door to eliminating womanhood altogether. Wollstonecraft repeats this key line several times in different ways in her work. She emphasizes the task to be performed: "I wish to shew that... the first object of laudable ambition is to obtain a character as a human being, regardless of the distinction of sex."[25] Elsewhere, she explains that women's education is less than par because the books are written by men who think of "females rather as women than human creatures."[26] The inference is the same: womanhood is something to be shunned while being a human creature in a generic and un-maternal form is to be embraced. Her effort seems innocent enough—she is trying to differentiate women from animals, or playthings. But over the generations, the idea will snowball, and down the road it transforms into something quite different than what Wollstonecraft may have intended, where the concept of woman is erased entirely.

Wollstonecraft was not shy about decrying the bonds of marriage, and with an understanding of her own parents' terrible relationship, it is not hard to see why this is so. For her, education was a way out that trumped and triumphed over anything that looked like submission, blind obedience, and abuse. In her work, however, the element of the tender and beautiful relationship that exists between husband and wife fails to come through with any clarity. Sarah Trimmer, another author who published with Joseph Johnson in London, whom Wollstonecraft held in great esteem, was critical of this gap in Wollstonecraft's work: "I can now say nothing more than that I found so much happiness in having a husband to assist me in forming a proper judgment, and in taking upon him the chief labour of providing for a family, that I never wished for a further degree of liberty or consequence than I enjoyed. Miss Woolstoncroft [sic] is a woman of extraordinary abilities, I confess; I cannot help thinking they might be employed to more advantage to society."[27] Perhaps if had Mary survived childbirth, her writings may have come to reflect the deeper goodness of marriage discovered in her relationship with William Godwin.

Legacy

From this basic sketch of Wollstonecraft, a simple foundation of feminism emerges. Although she didn't use the word "patriarchy" explicitly, her criticisms have been passed down through the generations with the effort to collapse hierarchies. She begins the neutering of the concept of female, driving it away from the maternal, and supplies the foundation for equating men and women in a way that denies any difference between the sexes.

Despite Mary's decreasing influence after her husband published her posthumous biography, her work maintained a place of primacy, as later feminists read her seminal work. Her work certainly isn't all bad. There are laudable elements in it, such as her desire for men to use more self-control and for women to reach their potential instead of remaining in a childish state, overly influenced by their own vanity, small appetites, and gossip. But there are elements in her life that are difficult to discern—for example, how committed she was to the ideals of what we now know as the free love movement, which sought to abolish monogamy, especially given her relationship with William Godwin.[28] Her real legacy beyond these small seeds was the family she left behind after her death, their integration of her work, and her keen absence. We know that her husband, and her future son-in-law poet, Percy Bysshe Shelley, were both free love proponents, the latter wreaking havoc among Mary's daughters, both Fanny and the future Mary Godwin Shelley. It is this aspect of her legacy that we will turn to next.

CHAPTER 2

Mary and the Romantics

It was a fall Saturday like any other, with families gathering to watch college football. And then a new ad came on. Pentagrams, vicious demons, graphic violence, grisly bodies, and headless chickens, all promoting the television series *Little Demon*. It wasn't another *Game of Thrones* spin-off but rather a series marketed to kids via the FX network, owned by none other than Disney. The network described the show as follows:

> 13 years after being impregnated by Satan, a reluctant mother, Laura, and her Antichrist daughter, Chrissy, attempt to live an ordinary life in Delaware, but are constantly thwarted by monstrous forces, including Satan, who yearns for custody of his daughter's soul.[1]

Danny DeVito plays the voice of the middle-aged, khaki-wearing Satan, just your average guy-next-door. This was presented during day-time hours of family viewing.

The satanic, the occult, and the esoteric have been swirling in our culture for a long time. It didn't start with the 1970s television series *Bewitched*. Its many sources have fueled a dramatic uptick in occult entertainment over the last several decades, found all over streaming networks, bookstores, and internet sites. Any trip to Barnes & Noble will confirm its influence with plentiful books on witchcraft, tarot cards, horoscope guides, and Ouija boards for sale.

In the 1980s, Madonna was at the forefront of the occult trend. She introduced iconoclastic pop paganism that desecrated the Virgin Mary, Christ, the saints, and the priesthood. Her songs, such as "Like a Virgin" and "Like a Prayer," profaned the sacred. But she took it to a new level in 2012 when she performed a Super Bowl halftime show riddled with satanic imagery. The lure of the occult in various media has given Wicca or witchcraft more adherents in the United States than there are members of the Presbyterian Church (PCUSA).[2]

The occult and the destruction of the patriarchy have gone hand in hand for centuries, as we will explore in this chapter. Madonna recently articulated this in a tweet:

> The Patriarchy continues to try to crush my neck with their heavy boots, cut off my life force and take away my voice—Even those who call themselves artists.............
> You know who you are!!! DEATH TO THE PATRIARCHY!
> Now and Forever.[3]

Clearly, a woman worth $850 million knows a thing or two about oppression. Now in her sixties and trying to stay relevant as a pop icon, Madonna was recently featured on a *Vanity Fair Italia* cover as the

Mother of Sorrows, a reference to the Virgin Mary, with the interior photos portraying her as Jesus Christ at the Last Supper surrounded by half-naked women at a bacchanal feast.[4]

It is no accident that Madonna has waded deep into both satanic rituals and feminism. Madonna and *Little Demon* illustrate the real occult influences in our culture. For generations these influences have been predominantly directed at women through witchcraft, but are now being aimed at younger and younger audiences.

Feminism has been deeply influenced by the occult, going back to its earliest stages. The source, in part, is connect to Mary Wollstonecraft's kin and legacy, particularly in the work of her daughter with William Godwin, Mary Godwin Shelley, author of *Frankenstein*, and son-in-law poet, Percy Bysshe Shelley. Percy Shelley, building in his own way on his mother-in-law's work, can rightfully claim Madonna as one of his intellectual offspring.

Romanticism

The intellectual stew that Wollstonecraft and her radical friends found themselves marinating in was a new movement called Romanticism. It was a reaction to the sterile reasoning espoused by Enlightenment thinkers. Kant and others ushered in the use of narrow categories of logic and reason to capture the expansiveness of reality, but there was simply too much left outside of these parameters. The Romantics saw the Enlightenment confines of reason as far too narrow, and they reacted with passion, emotion, creativity, and spontaneity. It was a reaction against laws, boundaries, scientism, and regimented ideas. It went deep into the hearts of those who wanted something wild, rule-breaking, romantic, creative, and liberating—especially sexually liberating.

Romanticism bloomed in full, developing ideas about faith, fancy, creation, and the meaning of human nature. There was one thing the

Romantics agreed with Enlightenment thinkers about: there was no longer room for Christianity. The Romantics were vehemently anti-Christian and saw freedom, no matter its expression, as their new creed. They challenged convention, broke taboos, and disrupted the status quo through prose, poetry, politicking, and profligate living.

Life after Mary's Death

After Mary Wollstonecraft's death, life continued for William Godwin. As an avowed atheist he refused to even attend his wife's funeral at Saint Pancras Church, believing strongly that there was no life after death. A few years later, he married a woman named Mary Jane Clairmont, with her two illegitimate children in tow, Charles and Jane. Their home was full with Godwin's two daughters, the new children, and later a son born to Godwin and Mary Jane.

Godwin's reputation as an anarchist was well established, and he enjoyed a measure of celebrity, hosting many notables in his home, including Aaron Burr after his notorious duel with Alexander Hamilton. Godwin's fame may have made it to France, with many of his ideas echoed in the work of the Marquis de Sade, although the evidence isn't clear. Writing at almost the same time, both men argued that marriage and convention only restricted man while throwing these off opens up the possibility of real freedom. Godwin's reputation would wain, while de Sade's much less developed political philosophy, peppered heavily with pornography, continued to influence major figures like Nietzsche, Jean-Paul Sartre, Simone de Beauvoir, and Kate Millett.

Financial troubles plagued the growing Godwin family, and William looked for creative ways to get out of debt and support his family. Percy Bysshe Shelley (1792–1822), who later became one of Godwin's intellectual disciples, introduced himself to Godwin and announced his sizable inheritance upon the death of his father. Godwin, seeing an opportunity for financial assistance, invited him to dinner. Anxious and intrigued to meet the daughter of the famous Mary Wollstonecraft and William Godwin, Shelley jumped at the chance. There at dinner, where all the Godwins were on their best behavior in hopes of extracting money from Shelley, Mary, Jane, and Fanny Godwin quickly fell in love with the charming Percy. And Percy, though already married, fell hard for Mary.

Shelley was the spoiled first son of a wealthy family with significant poetic talent, a wild streak, and a huge estate to inherit. Among his passions were women (often several at a time), fire, the occult and secret societies, and fast boats. He was a great playboy and dedicated atheist, expelled from Oxford for publishing the 1811 atheistic tract *The Necessity of Atheism.*

Percy and Mary, then just sixteen, would soon run off together to France, along with Mary's stepsister Jane, who would later change her name to Claire. Jane went along for the adventure but stayed for years when she too became part of the menage. The three rummaged their way around France and Switzerland, their money quickly running out. For all their hopes of a romantic getaway, their trip was anything but.

The trio returned to England. There the thorny issue of Percy's pregnant wife, Harriet Westbrook Shelley, and the couple's children had to be dealt with (Harriet eventually killed herself after Percy's abandonment). And then there was the ever-present question of money. Percy, Mary, and Jane found a residence together in London but moved frequently to avoid creditors. Eventually, Mary became pregnant, though their son died shortly after a premature birth. Percy and Mary were later married and welcomed three more children.

As time wore on, William Godwin cut a blustery figure, and again, as with his compromise in marrying a pregnant Mary Wollstonecraft, he didn't adhere to his principles when it came to his own family. He cut off direct communication to his daughter Mary for years after she ran off with the still-married Shelley, but he also didn't let the scandal of his daughter's affair preclude him from asking them for money. Later, the relationship between Godwin and his daughter would be restored, though it was always plagued by financial requests and demands.

Aside from the purse strings connecting the men, Godwin's work remained a lodestone for Shelley. He developed a great zeal for Godwin's idea of anarchy and the idea of casting off the constricting bonds of the family. In the meantime, inspired by Romantic ideals, Shelley developed the idea that poetry was a great source of knowledge and truth. Poetry, he believed, was both the creation and proof of one's sense of morality and compassion. Ironically, given his conviction that imagination made men moral, Shelley was a man of great imagination but not a man of great compassion.

"He, in the end," a biographer explained, "was a child of the European Enlightenment, and believed that the world could be revolutionized by language, and that fire was the element of imagination."[5] Interestingly, this idea of imagination and morality would resurface later, particularly in the 1960s, when conventions were abandoned and morality became synonymous with creativity, fueled by free love and drug use. Percy's life was marked by narcissism, and he left a trail of rancor and sadness in his wake, including deaths by suicide—both that of his first wife, Harriet, and then of Fanny, Mary Wollstonecraft's first daughter, who committed suicide after Percy seduced her. He fathered numerous illegitimate children and had a stream of creditors looking to collect on his debts. As a gifted poet, Shelley's influence was felt deeply by later thinkers, including the feminists. He wove together the thought of Godwin and Wollstonecraft in new and unique ways, including a new icon of womanhood—free from men and children—developed in his poetry that remains with us today.

Shelley's Satanic Feminism

During this era, reverence for science reached a fever pitch, with the expectation that scientific inquiry could discover the answers to every human need, even that of creating human life. Shelley was fascinated by electricity, fire, and their potential. Both Shelley and his wife Mary wrote on Prometheus, the Greek mythical character who brought man to life. Percy wrote in optimistic terms in *Prometheus Unbound*, while Mary, more pessimistic, wrote her best-known work *Frankenstein*, at just eighteen years old. Their interests in science, electricity, and the creation of life did not end there. "Like most intellectuals of the era," a biographer explained, "Shelley regarded science as a branch of philosophy, or sometimes as an offshoot of the occult. He searched for spirits as avidly as he stared through his solar microscope, studied chemistry even as he sought to summon the devil. One night, he sneaked into a church to spend the night in the burial vault, hoping to see ghosts."[6] Shelley's interest in the occult and the demonic was a theme in his work, especially in his interpretation of John Milton's poem *Paradise Lost*. Godwin before him had turned the Satan of Milton's design "into an embodiment of precisely the anarchist values he himself propagated. The rebellion against God turns into a reflection of his own hatred of illegitimate authority and inherited power."[7] Shelley went further, performing a subtle sleight of hand in his reading of a scene featured in that poem. When the serpent is tempting Eve, rather than casting the temptation as negative because the serpent is tricking Eve into disobedience, Shelley recasts it as an authentic opportunity for Eve: "Nothing," Shelley wrote, "can exceed the grandeur and the energy of the character of the Devil as expressed in Paradise Lost."[8] For him the serpent represents creativity, passion, and freedom: "Better to reign in Hell, than to serve in Heaven";[9] "Which way shall I fly / Infinite wrath and infinite despair? / Which way I fly is Hell; myself am Hell";[10] or "Evil be thou my good."[11] The doomed and evil Satan, the villain of Milton's *Paradise*

Lost, is for Shelley transformed into the ideal symbol of Romantic rebellion and freedom. Shelley viewed the diabolical passions as the opposite side of the typically masculine characteristics of order, reason, law, hierarchy, obedience, and authority. God, he believed, was the source of order and all that is male, while Satan, represented by the serpent, was the source of passion and creativity. Men and women, in his view, were not meant to be children of God, but rather opposing forces. "Woman and Satan are both part of nature," Per Faxneld, author of *Satanic Feminism: Lucifer as the Liberator of Women in Nineteenth-Century Culture*, explains, "while God and males are connected to a hierarchical, unjust civilization."[12]

Shelley's view, though certainly not exclusive to him, was in sharp contrast to the more traditional reading of Genesis 3. The traditional reading of Genesis 3 viewed Eve's disobedience as inverting the order of creation. God was the pinnacle, with Adam the head of the family and Eve as his helpmate, with humanity having dominion over the animals.[13] The Shelley reading of Genesis 3 makes the serpent (the animal) the highest authority, Eve next, with Adam last, and God ignored altogether.

Shelley built on the idea sparked by Milton's devil of restructuring society and inverting the moral order entirely. This inversion is in many respects what we're left with today: the decimation of the patriarchy and the male voice have inordinately enshrined the desires of women. In a later poem, *Revolt of Islam*, Shelley "made God the author of all evil and Satan the bringer of good,"[14] with Satan becoming "an icon of righteous revolt."[15] Shelley goes further, however, and solidifies the link between freedom-loving Satan and oppressed women, blending the work of Godwin and Wollstonecraft. In *Revolt of Islam*, the heroine is Cythna, "the earthly messenger of Satan the liberator. This messenger propagates feminist ideas and defies gender roles."[16] Cythna is the voice of the feminist revolution, following Satan, the liberator, and she asks rhetorically: "Can man be free if woman be a slave?"[17] In the end, Cythna liberates women by "disenchanting" them. As Faxneld writes, "Without being overly anachronistic, this can be read as a shattering of their false consciousness through subversion of myths (social and religious) that are their true fetters."[18] Or as Shelley put it, "I would only awaken the feelings, so that the reader should see the beauty of true virtue, and be incited to those inquiries which have led to my moral and political creed."[19] Shelley said he wrote Cythna "in the view of kindling within the bosoms of my readers a virtuous enthusiasm for...doctrines of liberty and justice."[20] And his view of liberty and justice was an effort "to create a counter-myth, a narrative that uses mythological figures to demonstrate certain ideological points (including explicitly feminist ones) in opposition to those typically inferred from the presently hegemonic myths of Christianity."[21] He used the devil and myths to create new narratives in the minds of readers, taking the place of earlier religious ideas. The Romantics knew that, in order to reshape culture, one had to go back to the beginning of culture and rewrite it.

With Cythna, Shelley created a new female archetype, the embodiment of the human creature that Mary Wollstonecraft idealized: the woman as an individual without any connection to motherhood, husbands, or children. The Victorian feminist Mathilde Blind (1841–1896) described "Cythna as 'a new female type' with no previous parallels in literature. All other poets creating fictional female figures, 'however pure or lofty these might be, had depicted her invariably in her relation as either wife or mistress, mother or daughter—that is a supplement to man's nature.'"[22] Cythna became the ideal individual, not connected to any kind of family, the model of womanhood. Her only real personal connection was with Satan. Shelley presciently saw that sex differences, what he called "detestable distinctions," would "surely be abolished in the future state of being."[23]

Mary's Creature

Mary Shelley is, of course, best known for her Gothic novel, *Frankenstein*. Dreamed up as part of a contest between her husband, her stepsister, Lord Byron, and a few others while in Italy, the story has become a classic. A scientist, Doctor Frankenstein, stitches together various body parts from the dead and is able to bring his "creature" to life. The creature, eight feet tall and hideous, just wants to be loved, but he is rejected by everyone, save a blind man who can't see his hideousness. Seeking revenge, the creature kills everyone whom Frankenstein loved, kills Frankenstein, and finally, in despair, kills himself, unloved and hopeless. There have been countless literary studies of this work, but one central theme is the radical idea that man can create life, that the spark of life can be found and used at will. This was a new notion, emerging after the Creator was purged from elite thinker's work, that mere humans could spark something so significant. Yet this created life isn't order and beauty and love, but truly the stuff of which nightmares are made.

But there is also something of a biographical element to this work. Mary Shelley knew that it was her birth that killed her mother. She felt removed from her father, partly because of his withdrawn character and later because of her relationship with Percy. For years, she was rejected and heard nothing but silence. The two people who should have been able to lavish her with love were not where they ought to have been. Her mother was in a graveyard, where Mary learned to write words by tracing the letters on Wollstonecraft's tombstone, and her father was at first distant and then effectively disowned her. In many respects, we can see Mary in the place of this lost creature who simply wants to be loved, as she followed Percy around Europe in much the same way the creature went to the ends of the earth to find Doctor Frankenstein.

There is also speculation that both the Shelleys read and were influenced by de Sade's work, books few would admit to having read.[24] It is known that Lord Byron had a copy of one of de Sade's books (*Justine*), so perhaps he shared them with his dear friends. Some have argued that a turn in Percy Shelley's work to torture and viciousness could signal de Sade's influence. De Sade was called "the freest spirit that ever lived." Shelley's life was a constant straining toward that same spirit.[25]

There appears to be more evidence of de Sade's influence upon Mary Shelley. There are several concurrent themes in de Sade's work and *Frankenstein*, many too nuanced to go into in this work, but the most obvious connection is the name Justine. *Justine, or The Misfortunes of Virtue*, was published by de Sade in 1792, while *Frankenstein* also had a tragic Justine, who is killed by Frankenstein's creature. The women in *Frankenstein*, one commentator noted, "like the women in Sade's books . . . are helpless. Indeed, it is possible that Shelley chose the name Justine for this hapless victim as an allusion to Sade's *Justine*."[26]

The Shelley Legacy

"I always go on until I am stopped," asserted Shelley, "and I never am stopped."[27] But in 1822, Shelley was stopped, when he died in a boating accident at the age of twenty-nine. He had been exiled in Italy for some time, his name so synonymous with lewd sexual scandal that he was scarcely mentioned in good English society. Later, the scent of scandal would be forgotten and his poetry would hold a place with the great English poets of the day, along with John Keats, William Blake, and Lord Byron. In contrast to his public reception, Mary Shelley's admiration for her husband never waned. Shortly after his death, she hinted that he was angelic and later wrote of his goodness much more boldly: "His spirit gathers peace in its new state from the sense that . . . his exertions were not made in vain, and in the progress of the liberty he so fondly loved. . . . It is our best consolation to know that such a pure-minded and exalted being was once among us, and now exists where we hope to one day join him...."[28] Mary would continue to publish books and saw her son Percy F. Shelley take over the family estate. The parallels between Mary and her mother are striking, as one biographer made clear:

> Both mother and daughter attempted to free themselves from the stranglehold of polite society, and both struggled to balance their need for love and companionship with their need for independence. They braved the criticism of their peers to write works that took on the most volatile issues of the day. Brave, passionate, and visionary, they broke almost every rule there was to break. Both had children out of wedlock. Both fought against the injustices women faced and both wrote books that revolutionized history.[29]

Mary continued to publish her own works, along with many of Percy's poems, although she had to do it anonymously because of the terms placed upon her by Shelley's father—terms she was required to keep in order for her son Percy to inherit his family's estate. After finally inheriting the family estate, Percy's wife, Jane, would be the one to scour Mary Shelley's diaries and make them readable for the public.

Mary and Claire's Regret

Free love, outside the boundaries of marital monogamy, was a significant theme in the work of most of the Romantics. Godwin spoke about how he thought marriage and family inhibited men and enslaved women. Shelley, with his libertine attitudes, made Godwin's ideas his own in both theory and practice.

Mary Shelley followed in her mother's footsteps, allowing her heart to go where it willed, unbound by any convention. "Always her mother's daughter," one biographer wrote, "she believed she and Percy could make their own rules. Later, Shelley would capture her words in his poem *Rosalind and Helen*, in which Mary's alter ego, Helen, tells her lover, 'But our church shall be the starry night, / Our altar the grassy earth outspread, / And our priest the muttering wind.'"[30]

Free love, for Shelley and Godwin—like Mary Wollstonecraft before them—was a key to living fully. Like Rousseau, they saw the confines of society as enslaving, and it was liberty of the individual—meaning the capacity to do anything that did not harm another—that would lead to a virtuous state. The dictates of the Church and superstition were confining, while nature and the pursuit of passions would lead to authentic men and women.

Despite Mary Shelley's final words of praise for her husband, there were times when she doubted the cost his demands extracted from her. There were moments, captured in letters, that reveal the heartache that came with their libertine life. In 1818, Mary and Percy had two living children, ten-month-old Clara and three-year-old William, lovingly referred to as "Wilmouse." Within a five-month period, both children would be dead: Clara first from a fever that she couldn't overcome when her mother went to Venice at Percy's bidding, and William of malaria picked up in Rome, after the family failed to leave the city despite being warned about the disease. Mary wondered if loving Percy came at too high a cost, especially when she remembered her lost children. She thought of herself as a curse, first causing her mother's death in childbirth and then unable to keep her own children alive. Mary's grief was agonizing. Paraphrasing from Mary's letters to friends, biographer Charlotte Gordon wrote that what Mary really wanted was to have her child back again, to hear his voice. She continues:

> If only she could hold him in her lap once again, show him
> the bright globes of lemons hanging on the trees, brush his

hair off his forehead, listen to him prattle about the birds and the flowers, go for walks near the cornfields, laugh at his pranks. She wanted to see him run down the lane. She wanted to hear him call her name. She wanted to feel his hand in hers.[31]

After these crushing deaths, her father warned her against becoming too hardened against Shelley, knowing of his capacity to seek out other women and fearing he would leave Mary as he had left others.

Mary is not the only one who lamented the steep cost of free love. Claire Claremont, the third of the Shelley trio who moved everywhere with them (and who was involved sexually with Percy and Mary) was also terribly damaged by free love put into practice. The jealous Claire decided at one point that she could finally outdo her stepsister by becoming the lover of the more famous poet Lord Byron, instead of just serving Percy, who was little known and scandal-ridden. Claire triumphed, eventually bore his daughter, whom she later gave to him to support, knowing he would be able to give her a much better life than she could. Tragically, their daughter Allegra died of typhus when she was five years old. It took everything Claire had to give Allegra to Byron, knowing she would be apart from her for most of her life, but her premature death was far worse. The pursuit of raw passions had left Claire destitute and broken. Gordon writes:

> Although she could not know it then—she was too grief-stricken, too stunned by pain to know exactly what she thought—for Claire, Allegra's death was a turning point. She and Mary had staked their lives on Shelley's ideals of free love, but when, at the end, she stood back and assessed what she had suffered—indeed what they all had suffered—she

decided that she, Mary, little Allegra, Harriet, Jane Williams, and all the other women Byron and Shelley had known and claimed to love had been gravely harmed by the men's deluded ideals. The two great poets had inflicted unspeakable pain, she believed, all in the name of freedom and passion. The loss of Allegra was the case in point. Her daughter was the sacrificial lamb in the Romantic experiment, the little girl who had been worth nothing in the eyes of her father.[32]

Despite the lofty and scintillating Romantic ideals, Mary and Claire endured the agonizing pain from the clash of their hopes with biological and emotional realities. As a result, near the end of her life, Claire wrote a denunciation of the two poets who had in some way ruined her life:

> Under the influence of the doctrine and belief of free love I saw the two first poets of England…become monsters of lying, meanness[,] cruelty and treachery—under the influence of free love Lord B became a human tyger slaking his thirst for inflicting pain upon defenceless women who under the influence of free love…loved him.[33]

A tidy picture of Shelley and Byron's path of destruction was summed up nicely by *New York Times* writer Ben Downing:

> Shelley's abandoned first wife committed suicide, and all but one of the four children he had with his second wife, Mary, died young. Claire Clairmont, meanwhile, had the daughter she'd conceived with Byron imperiously stripped from her by the poet, who, quickly tiring of the girl, stuffed her in a

convent, where she too soon died. There was also a baby of mysterious parentage, registered as Elena Shelley, who survived only 18 months. In short, the two poets left the Italian peninsula, along with a few spots in England, strewn with dead relations. While they cannot entirely be blamed, it's hard not to conclude that their callousness, selfishness, impulsiveness and bullying demand for "free love" were ruinous to those around them.[34]

It is a curious thing to see the potency that this small family unleashed into the world. Their ideas would act, like a poisoned bouillon cube, seeping out to the wider culture. We can see traces of their emphasis on the power to create, reinvent, and carve out a life away from any traditional mores and conventions. Tragically, despite the Shelleys' and their friend's best efforts to deny, or somehow move beyond, what they considered outmoded behavior, they continually fell in the traps of the body and nature that marriage is meant to protect against. They lived with a kind of hubris believing that they were new and radical by defying convention. History, of course, shows that they were not so novel, but what was novel, as we shall see, was Shelley's development of the character of Cythna, who would become a model for future generations seeking to define a new kind of woman devoid of family relationships.

In *The Gay Science*, written in 1882, the German philosopher Friedrich Nietzsche proclaimed that "God is dead!...And we have killed him."[35] The oft-quoted segment from the oft-quoted philosopher describes a European civilization where Enlightenment rationalism had made God intentionally obsolete. It was a world ready to embrace "new values." In early nineteenth-century Europe this seems to have taken two forms: to see man as merely matter, and (perhaps paradoxically) as the measure of all things, or else to embrace the occult and esoteric, a new superstition in the face of the old. Just as the Terror did not remain only in France, what happened in England did not stay in England. This European innovation was about to gain a global reach.

CHAPTER 3

Elizabeth and Seneca's Fall

Elizabeth Cady Stanton (1815–1902) and Susan B. Anthony (1820–1906) have long been heralded as the foundresses of the women's movement in the United States.[1] Today, the Smithsonian Museum in Washington, D.C., features the mahogany Spirit Table, made famous as the place where Stanton wrote her "Declaration of Sentiments," the women's movement's *cri de coeur* for suffrage. Most depictions of Stanton sound something like this:

> Stanton powerfully captured the personal drama inherent in the public event, and her account has dominated historical narratives ever since. Using her own life as a lens, Stanton connected everyday events, grounded in personal relationships, with the meaning of American democracy itself. In so doing, she validated not only her own experience but the experience of women everywhere, not simply in their roles as daughters,

wives, and mothers but as individual human beings. More
than a mere historical document, Stanton's story is so compelling that it has assumed the status of a myth.[2]

Descriptions of Stanton as courageous, brilliant, and edifying
abound. She and Anthony are portrayed as hard-working visionaries,
the right women for the right time, leading others to a more promising
land. There are, however, a few flies in the ointment of this portrayal.
During their own time, Stanton worked hard to craft the myth that she
and Anthony were the first and only pioneers of the women's movement,
stories which are often taken as orthodoxy today among feminists. But
a deeper look reveals darker shades of their tale.[3] Moreover, there seem
to have been efforts made to keep what might appear to be unsavory
details about these two women out of their legacies. The personal
papers of Susan B. Anthony were burned by her biographer, Ida Husted
Harper,[4] and numerous biographies of the two do not touch upon the
occult elements of their story, with many details whitewashed, including
those behind the famous Smithsonian Spirit Table. Stanton has long
been considered the intellectual engine between the two, with Anthony
serving more as her mouthpiece since she was single and able to travel,
unlike Stanton, who was busy at home with her large family. This
chapter will look at details that reflect a different image of Stanton and
her role in shaping the women's movement.

As with the previous chapter, many of the events during this time
were not prim and proper. Instead, they capture a raw period of U.S.
history. The ideas expounded by Wollstonecraft, Godwin, and Shelley
found a foothold during this period, and were expanded in new and
salacious ways. Antebellum New York State seemed to be the heart of it
all. It was the heart of the Second Great Awakening and the spiritualist
movement, which would sweep the country with a crazed and zealous
religious fervor. New York was also a privileged place for prostitution,

with elegant brothels dotting the city, and at least one busy and illegal abortion clinic. *The Gentlemen's Guide*, a popular travel guide at the time, listed a brothel visit as a regular part of a gentleman's evening out. After the Civil War, prostitution surged in New York City, with over twenty thousand women involved in the industry.[5] Southern women, who had lost homes and husbands, needed work to keep them from starving. This was the backdrop to the budding women's movement.

Stanton's Early Life

Elizabeth Cady Stanton was born into an upper class family to Daniel and Margaret Livingston Cady in 1815. Her father was a warm and kindly judge; her mother was quite different. "Almost six feet tall," she was described as "stern—an imposing, dominant, and vivacious figure who controlled the Cady household with a firm hand. Stanton would later describe her as... 'inclined to a stern military rule of the household.'"[6] Elizabeth chafed against her parents' authority, particularly that of her mother. Her parents were strict Calvinists, and Stanton often found herself living in terror of losing her soul, running to her father for consolation.

Although Elizabeth was closest to her father, he often lamented that she had been born a girl. In 1826, when Stanton was eleven years old, the family lost its first-born son, Eleazar, at the age of twenty-one. Elizabeth was determined to become the son for which her father longed. "Her own struggle against parental authority now became a struggle to please that authority," one commentator explained. "She knew how desperately he wanted a son. She knew she could never be that son. But she also knew that, if she tried, she could do everything that boys could do, and often she could do it better."[7]

But Elizabeth, although successful in school, was prohibited from going to college, which was limited to men at the time. She did attend a kind of women's seminary and later clerked for her father. She would eventually fall in love with her older sister's husband, Edward Bayard, and he with her. Knowing that any kind of relationship would cast them out of polite society and be a great betrayal to her family, Elizabeth found another diversion in abolitionist Henry Stanton, who, like Bayard, was ten years older than her and very intellectual. Though many in the family disapproved of the match, doubting that Henry Stanton would amount to much financially, Elizabeth and Henry married in a hurry, partially to avoid what Elizabeth felt was backsliding toward her brother-in-law.

While honeymooning in London, Henry attended an abolitionist meeting. Women were required to sit away from the proceedings, which enraged Elizabeth. Her vexation at the double standard for men and woman stirred up afresh her regret at not being male.

Eventually, Henry and Elizabeth would set up their first home in Seneca Falls. There are often references to the misery Elizabeth felt, living in Seneca Falls and raising her children, especially her first three sons, while Henry was on the road. Elizabeth spoke of "mental hunger" and a need for intellectual stimulation. As most women with small children can understand, this is a difficult reality, but Elizabeth did have maids at her disposal and was able to spend long periods of time in the upper class comforts of her paternal home. Moreover, Elizabeth didn't always bristle at homemaking. Shortly after she was married, she spoke of the delight she felt to be the mistress of her own home. "With two servants, she ran her household with 'that same feeling of pride and satisfaction that a young minister must have in taking charge of his first congregation.' She was a perfectionist, and the smallest tasks inspired her to excellence. 'I studied up everything pertaining to housekeeping,' she remembered, 'and enjoyed it all.'"[8] Stanton went on:

> Even washing day—that day so many people dread—had its charms for me. The clean clothes on the lines and on the

grass looked so white, and smelled so sweet, that it was a pretty sight to contemplate. I inspired my laundress with an ambition to have her clothes look white and to get them out earlier than our neighbors, and to have them ironed and put away sooner.[9]

She was inspired by both cooking and cleaning. From her love of homemaking emerged "love of order and cleanliness," even to the extent of giving a man "an extra shilling to pile the logs of firewood with their smooth ends outward, though I did not have them scoured white, as did our Dutch grandmothers." Like an artist, she was creating a "clean, orderly, beautiful" home.[10]

But at some point, homemaking lost its shine for Stanton, and she grew bored with the effort. "I now fully understood the practical difficulties most women had to contend with in the isolated household, and the impossibility of woman's best development if in contact, the chief part of her life, with servants and children." Stanton continued:

> The general discontent I felt with women's portion as wife, mother, housekeeper, physician, and spiritual guide, the chaotic condition into which everything fell without her constant supervision, and the wearied, anxious look of the majority of women, impressed me with the strong feeling that some active measures should be taken to remedy the wrongs of society in general and of women in particular.[11]

Elizabeth longed for something more intellectual as well as for a husband to be home to help shoulder the load. The women's movement was her way out. As time wore on, Henry Stanton's absence continued, and eventually he became less supportive of Elizabeth's work, straining their marriage.

Meanwhile, Elizabeth continued to have affection for her brother-in-law. "Many years later, Stanton's daughter, Harriot Stanton Blatch, agreed that 'yes, no doubt my mother was as much in love with Edward Bayard as he was with her.'"[12] Elizabeth later confessed that, even after seven children and as many years of marriage, "she was still in love with Edward Bayard and to him went 'the steadfastness of my affection.' Elizabeth was to say that instead of 'seeking solace elsewhere' she had channeled her energies into the fight for woman's rights."[13] She was motivated by the person she could never be for her father, the wife and homemaker she could never be for her husband, and the lover she could never be for her brother-in-law.

Spiritualism

Little sense can be made of Elizabeth Stanton's work without digging into spiritualism, an outgrowth of America's Second Great Awakening. Over time, Stanton renounced allegiance to any specific Christian church, growing away from her early Calvinism and toward spiritualism and even secularism or agnosticism. She would later become involved in the Free Religion advocates, which "aspired to be an active national force dedicated to the secularization of the United States."[14] But prior to that, spiritualism was unfolding in front of her very eyes.

This period in U.S. history was a time of spiritual revival, though it came in unusual and unorthodox flavors. On some level, the Second Great Awakening, burgeoning under free thinkers and denominations such as the Quakers and the Shakers, was a driver of spiritual piety, but in other ways it was a match to the flame of free love, a movement promoting sexual relationships beyond monogamy, and occult activities. It had explicit, though not readily discussed, sexual elements, melding together the sexual and the spiritual, with some big-tent revivals turning into orgiastic romps in place of modern-day altar calls. These revivals also included many occult practices, such as séances, fortune telling, and connecting with spirits on "the other side." It was this last element—where mediums, predominantly women, would speak to the spirit world—that would come to be known as spiritualism.

Confidence in science and electricity was at an all-time high. The country was changing quickly from an agrarian outpost to a highly industrialized commercial leader. Telegraphs were being installed around the growing country, connecting people in ways never seen as possible before. Like the telegraph, a new technology connecting one place to the next, the medium of a spiritualist connected this world to the next. Some called it a "spiritual telegraph." Demand was high to reach out to those who had died, given high morbidity rates among children from disease and later from the high casualties of the Civil War. Cholera was a frequent killer, with many dying quickly, within twelve hours of contracting the horrendous disease.

Spiritualism began in 1848 at the Fox family home in Hydesville, New York, where odd sounds were heard. The eldest daughter, Kate Fox, appeared to have communicated with the spirits in the home, who responded with raps on a table. The spirits' raps seemed to answer correctly when questioned about such queries as the ages of people in the room. Word spread quickly of the odd phenomenon, and soon the members of the Fox family had to take refuge somewhere else, but the rapping came with them. It was believed that certain tables could transmit the spirits' messages. These became known as "spirit tables."

Spiritualism spread like wildfire. Estimates have ranged from two million adherents before the Civil War to close to seven million after. "Judging from its rapid extension and widespread effects," a reporter from the *New York Times* wrote, "it seems to be the new Mahomet, or the social Antichrist, overrunning the world."[15]

Although spiritualism appeared to emerge from various denominations of Christianity, it was generally not considered Christian. In fact, it was an inversion of many of Christianity's tenants. No male clergy was necessary, most of the engagement happened at home rather than church, and organized religion became unnecessary because of the authority given to the spirits. Among "the spiritualists' church, so-called," a Methodist writer noted that "women are the high-priests; and the scriptural teachings in regard to the relation of men and women and their duties are reversed."[16]

Adherents, called spiritualists, had free-thinking ideas and often disdained Christianity. Spiritualism had an air of sophistication, unmoored from what was generally and ironically called superstition. For the cosmopolitan it was a tantalizing DIY approach to faith which offered proof of the other side, something Christianity could not do, without the confines of traditional morality. This unmooring, in addition to promoting women's rights, permitted the growth of the free love movement. Casting off dogmas and laws, encouraged by the spirits, marriage and family were abandoned as great evils, replaced by the virtues of free love. These adherents continued to be inspired by Mary Wollstonecraft, William Godwin, and both Percy and Mary Shelley. Stanton's own work was indebted to them.[17]

Spiritualism and women's rights became tightly woven together. One commentator explained:

> Spiritualism and woman's rights drew from the same well:
> Both were responses to the control, subjugation, and repression of women by church and state. Both believed in universal suffrage—the equality of all human beings. For women—sheltered, repressed, powerless—the line between divine inspiration, the courage of one's convictions, and spirit guidance became blurred. Not all woman's rights

advocates became Spiritualists, but Spiritualism embraced woman's rights.[18]

Spiritualism, feminism, and free love emerged as part of a new trinity of salvation:

> Feminism—the infidelity to male supremacy—officially began as an organized movement at Seneca Falls, New York, in 1848: spiritualism—the direct communication with the spirit world which profoundly subverted organized religion—began with the Fox family rappings in Hydesville, New York, in 1848; and free love—the infidelity to the primary social institution, the family—began in the same general area and time.[19]

These three elements, homegrown in New York, worked in tandem, and anyone during that era who considered themselves a radical was involved in all three.[20]

The Spirit Table and the Declaration of Sentiments

One biographer dismisses the influence of spiritualism on Stanton, summarizing Elizabeth's position as skeptical.[21] But any skepticism she may have had seems to have dissipated with her own experiences with spiritualism, mediums, and spirit tables. "Spiritualism," wrote a biographer, "and the inception of woman's rights were inextricably intertwined. Elizabeth Cady Stanton heard spirit raps in her home. And when Gerrit Smith's daughter Elizabeth (Libby) Smith came for a visit, she too heard them."[22] An acquaintance of Stanton's described the influence of belief in spirits on the early women's rights advocates:

As to the rapping heard at Rochester and which I heard when
then away from the [Fox] girls…I hear it very frequently, and
much more now than then.…Thomas McClintock's folks are
very sure that they have heard the same. Also Elisabeth [sic]
Stanton. Gerrit Smith's daughter was on a visit to E. Stanton
and heard about it. She went home and told her mother who
had full faith in it and the daughter wrote to E. Stanton, a
day or two since, that her mother had heard it several times
so if it is Humbug it seems to spread fast.[23]

As mentioned in this missive, the Thomas M'Clintock family
appeared to have one of these famed spirit tables. It was around this
that Stanton and her friends found the needed inspiration for their
Seneca Falls conference:

Just one month after the three-legged spirit table in the
McClintocks' parlor reverberated with raps as the Waterloo
Congregational Friends were formulating their declaration
of principles, Elizabeth Cady Stanton and four other women
assembled in the same parlor to discuss the plight of women.
Three of these women—Mary Ann McClintock, Lucretia
Mott, and Jane Hunt—were Waterloo Congregational
Friends.…To these women Elizabeth Cady Stanton, a frustrated thirty-three-year-old mother of three sons, "poured
out…the torrent of my long-accumulating discontent with
such vehemence and indignation that I stirred myself, as well
as the rest of the party, to do or dare anything." Stanton
wrote that she and the other women were determined to call
a "convention to discuss the social, civil, and religious condi-
tion and rights of women," to be held July 19 and 20 in the
Wesleyan Chapel in Seneca Falls, New York.[24]

The women felt like they needed some sort of a declaration or manifest around which to focus the conference:

> It was essential that they prepare a statement of their beliefs, but Stanton said she and her companions "felt as helpless and hopeless as if they had been suddenly asked to construct a steam engine." Lucretia Mott, a well-known Quaker preacher and abolitionist, was the only one who had any experience as an organizer. The rest of the women were occupied solely as wives and mothers. Reports from antislavery and temperance conventions were suggested as models for their declaration, but these documents seemed dull and imprecise. Time grew short until only five days remained before the convention, and still no paper had been written. Stanton, desperately seeking inspiration, sat down at the McClintocks' spirit table, picked up the Declaration of Independence, and began reading it aloud. At once the women decided to use it as the basis for their own Declaration of Rights and Sentiments. "We hold these truths to be self-evident, that all men *and women* are created equal...." Miraculously, the ideas began to flow as Elizabeth Cady Stanton placed her paper on the spirit table and wrote the declaration for "the first organized protest against the injustice which has brooded for ages over the character and destiny of one-half the race."[25]

Inspired, they called their manifest the Declaration of Sentiments, based on the Declaration of Independence, but with "women" inserted into the document. "The new document captured their imaginations. It also captured the spirit of a generation. It would be the single most important factor in spreading news of the woman's rights movement around the country in 1848 and into the future."[26]

But how would these upper class women articulate grievances against men the way the colonists had listed their grievances against King George III? Despite their source of inspiration, their grievances were hardly the same as the colonists against the British crown. They enlisted help from the men to enumerate what less fortunate women might have felt. "After hours of diligent searching, of creeds, codes, customs and constitutions," Stanton remembered, "we were rejoiced to find that we could make out as good a bill of impeachment against our sires and sons as they had against old King George."[27] Charles M'Clintock, noticing the amount of time it was taking, quipped, "Your grievances must be very grievous indeed, if it takes you so long to find them."[28]

Of course, the Declaration of Sentiments and the Seneca Falls conference were a huge success and set off a ripple effect around the country, with women's groups cropping up and legislation making its way into law to protect the needs and rights of women. Stanton and the other conference organizers believed firmly they were creating "the greatest revolution the world has ever seen."[29] They were not mistaken.

Theosophy and *The Woman's Bible*

Having abandoned the Christian faith of her childhood, Stanton took it upon herself to try to eradicate the faith that she felt was the source of women's enslavement. She and other women wrote their own Bible, calling it *The Woman's Bible*, a book that turned much of the biblical story on its head while presenting a new myth of women's proper origin.

Some of the influence on *The Woman's Bible* was from the movement known as theosophy. A close cousin of spiritualism, theosophy included mediums and contacts with "the other side" but also went deeper into spiritual texts and traditions from around the world. The movement was founded by Helena Petrovna Blavatsky (1831–1891), a Russian noble who ran away after being married at sixteen. She traveled the world, supporting herself as a medium. She studied voodoo, Native American spirituality, and Buddhism in Tibet. Her influence spread among artists and writers, suffragettes and socialists, including Wassily Kandinsky, W. B. Yeats, and Paul Klee.

Theosophy was a loose-enough concept to accommodate most progressive efforts, including "feminism, socialism, vegetarianism, anti-imperialism, and anti-war efforts. Many individuals participating in these efforts were anticlerical or even anti-Christian. Blavatsky's pro-Satan provocations fit well into this context."[30] Stanton was certainly not the last feminist to be influenced by theosophy; it maintained an underground type of existence for decades. Gloria Steinem referenced her own mother engaging in theosophy in the 1960s, when it enjoyed a resurgence among the free love, feminist, "abandon authority" crowd.[31]

One of Blavatsky's ideas, and the thread picked up by Stanton, was to put forward a "Satanic counter-myth to attack the patriarchal use of traditional Bible readings to keep women in their place."[32] The Bible, according to theosophy, was not a divine text but a historic one that propped up men's oppression of women. "Blavatsky's view of the Fall as a positive, gnosis-bringing event thus implicitly becomes an up-valuation of women: she is no longer responsible for mankind's fall into sin but is instead actively involved in the gaining of spiritual wisdom from the benevolent snake."[33]

The Woman's Bible was written to show that there are many ways to read the Bible, especially from a feminist point of view. Stanton was deeply interested in theosophy, speaking of her enthusiasm for it in her 1898 autobiography, *Eighty Years and More*. Three of the contributors to *The Woman's Bible* also considered themselves theosophists. Theosophy's fingerprints can be seen in this work. In the introduction to *The Woman's Bible*, Stanton declares church and clergy "the very powers that make her [women's] emancipation impossible."[34] She adds that "[women's] political and social degradation are but an outgrowth of your status in the Bible."[35] Faxneld writes:

> Fall or no Fall, Stanton proceeds to praise Eve…proclaiming she is "pleased with her attitude, whether as a myth in an allegory, or as the heroine of an historical occurrence" and that "the unprejudiced reader must be impressed with the courage, the dignity, and the lofty ambition of the woman." Satan, she says, "evidently had a profound knowledge of human nature, and saw at a glance the high character of the person he met," since he tempted her with "knowledge, the wisdom of the Gods." She next likens Satan to Socrates or Plato, since "his powers of conversation and asking puzzling questions, were no doubt marvelous, and he roused in the woman that intense thirst for knowledge."[36]

Like Shelley before her, Stanton doesn't debunk the Christian myth of the Fall; she creates a new counter-myth: "Stanton explained a dramatic implication of her deconstruction of Genesis 3: 'Take the snake, the fruit tree and the woman from the tableau, and we have no fall, nor frowning judge, no Inferno, no everlasting punishment—hence no need for a Savior.'"[37] She provided "a counter-myth where Eve is a heroine and Satan a charitable philosophical instructor of woman." There is speculation that Stanton didn't inherit this idea solely from Blavatsky, but also from other Romantic poets. "In her biography, Stanton likens herself to Shelley when he was scattering one of his suppressed pamphlets. Later, she describes Shelley as 'a sensitive, refined nature, full of noble purposes.' One should perhaps not make too much of it, but it is a possibility that Stanton's counter-myths with didactic purposes were to some degree inspired by Shelley's similar endeavours in texts like *The Revolt of Islam*."[38]

Upon publication, Stanton discovered that not everyone was as much of a fan of Shelley and Blavatsky, or of the idea that the snake of Genesis 3 was a kindly benefactor. As a result of her radical theology, Stanton was disowned by the major U.S. suffrage organization, the National American Woman Suffrage Association (NAWSA), of which she was the honorary president. The dustup over *The Woman's Bible*, however, was nothing compared to what would come next.

The Final Fall from Grace

The growing women's movement would hit a significant snag, splintering it into two camps. The movement had grown piggybacking upon the abolitionist movement. One commentator posited that it was a natural connection because of the belief that "women and slaves suffered from the same oppressor—the white male."[39]

After the Civil War, the question of voting rights for newly freed male slaves was a hot political issue. For Stanton, the question of allowing ignorant slaves to vote before educated women was a slap in the face. "Think of Patrick and Sambo and Hans and Yung Tung, who do not know the difference between a monarchy and a republic, who cannot read the Declaration of Independence or Webster's spelling book, making laws for Lucretia Mott...[or] Susan B. Anthony," she wrote, revealing her elitist attitude.[40]

Eventually, two groups would form because of Stanton's racist position. In Boston, the American Woman Suffrage Association (AWSA) was formed in 1869 and supported African-American men's right to vote granted in the Fifteenth Amendment.[41] The AWSA was also made up of both men and women with a focus on suffrage for women.

Stanton's group, the National Woman Suffrage Association (NWSA), was made up of women, considered a broad range of women's issues, and bristled against black men getting to vote before white women.

This rift over the Fifteenth Amendment created tension between the groups as they vied for media attention, especially on the twenty-fifth anniversary of Seneca Falls. With well-known journalists on their side, the AWSA had become the public favorite. In an effort to regain some of their prestige, Stanton and Anthony grasped at straws. They lined up the presidential candidate Victoria Woodhull, "a woman no one could ignore."[42]

Perhaps more than any other woman, Victoria was the embodiment of the new trinity: a feminist, spiritualist, and free love advocate all rolled into one a very colorful package. Some called her the "Joan of Arc of the Women's Movement," while others called her the "Prostitute Who Ran for President." Woodhull was considered the free love "high priestess." Susan B. Anthony called her a "bright, glorious, young and strong spirit," while Stanton believed that "in the annals of emancipation the name [Victoria Woodhull] will have its own high place as a deliverer."[43]

Woodhull, born Victoria Claflin, grew up with her sister Tennessee Claflin during the Great Awakening, daughters of a ne'er-do-well snake-oil salesman, Buck Claflin. The large Claflin family was constantly on the road, running from authorities from town to town for outrageous levels of fraud. Victoria and Tennessee, engaged in the fraud from the earliest of ages, were cash cows for the family as mediums, working at revivals and fairs. Another of Buck Claflin's enterprises was the curing of cancer, where he applied lye directly to the skin of sufferers, leading many to excruciatingly painful and premature deaths. No scheme was too far-fetched for the Claflin family, and prostitution and fortune telling by his many daughters seemed to be a mainstay.

Victoria said that to speak of her life without talking about her *spirits*, was like "writing *Hamlet* and decid[ing] to leave out his father's ghost."⁴⁴ She made many of her decisions based on the advice of spirits, particularly one she claimed was named Demosthenes. Her first escape was to marry Canning Woodhull, with whom she had two children, Byron, named for Lord Byron, and Zulu. They divorced and she later married and divorced Colonel James Blood.

Eventually, to escape their abusive family and the authorities (Tennessee was wanted for manslaughter related to the cancer-curing scheme), Victoria and Tennessee made their way to New York City and were introduced to Cornelius Vanderbilt, who was interested in connecting with the spirits for profits. Sure enough, Victoria's spirits gave him advice that made him money, solidifying their relationship, while Tennessee became his favored concubine. As his pockets were filled with the Woodhull's spiritualist advice, Vanderbilt decided it could be lucrative to establish for the sisters their own brokerage firm, so in 1870, the sisters had the first female firm. They also started a weekly newspaper called *Woodhull and Claflin's Weekly*, where they spoke of such things as free love, local gossip, and investing.

Although a bit leery of Victoria and Tennie's reputation, the Woodhull dollars proved to be just too attractive for Stanton and Anthony to turn down, so they joined forces. The feisty Woodhull spoke at their event. Although her speech was stirring and met with significant applause, her free love message would soon put Stanton and Anthony in an awkward mess. The women of the AWSA pounced on Woodhull's scandalous speech. Stanton was livid at their hypocrisy for she knew too well that many of the men and women in the AWSA were engaging in free love lifestyles.

Victoria, never far from scandal, was also livid with the public response. Aware of a particular free love relationship involving the best-known preacher in America, Victoria splashed details of the affair across *Woodhull and Claflin's Weekly.*[45]

The scandal involved Henry Ward Beecher and his protégé, Theodore Tilton, married to Elizabeth "Lib" Tilton. Beecher had seduced Tilton's wife, Lib. Tilton, who was very committed to free love, had initially been unperturbed by the relationship and thought extending his free love liberties to his wife could be a good thing. Their relationship would be one of "loving friends," which would allow both to pursue others at will. Tilton even introduced Lib to one of his numerous mistresses, who would come and go from their home. All that changed dramatically when he realized that the baby his wife was carrying was likely not his own. This stirred up a rage that destroyed what was left of the marriage, and nearly crushed his wife:

> Lib Tilton knew full well that the life she carried within her was about to be expunged. No one wanted it—not her husband, or her preacher, or his wife.... One morning she felt an uncontrollable urge to flee....
>
> On the eighth, or perhaps the tenth day of her isolation, for she had lost track of the days, she saw that the sky was clear and a light snow had descended. Once more she donned her cloak and pulled the hood over her head to conceal her face. Now Lib knew where she was going. . . . At noon she arrived at the Greenwood Cemetery and made her way to the place where her children, Paul and Mattie, were buried in the frozen earth. "Such tiny graves," she thought, and sank to her knees, then spread her body across the cold earth as if to warm the graves of her children. She lay there "and felt peace." She knew not how long it was before she felt a rough hand grasp her shoulder. "Get up, girl," commanded the groundskeeper.

"There's no place for you here." Lib did not move. "Get up, do you hear me!" he said, and began to shake her.

Lib Tilton stood. "If there is one spot on earth that is mine, it is these two graves," she said. The groundskeeper regarded her soberly, then removed his hat and bowed his head. "I did not know they were yours," he said. He turned and left. Lib recalled, "I stayed there lying on the little graves all the rest of the day."[46]

A few days later, she aborted her child. Like the Shelleys before them, the Tiltons felt the hard edge of the free love lifestyle, an edge no one had considered until a child no one wanted was conceived. The ripples of the Tilton's free love arrangement wouldn't end there.

Woodhull's publication of all the details of Beecher's seduction of Lib Tilton led to a public trial between Tilton and Beecher. Lines were drawn between their supporters, including Beecher's sister, Harriet Beecher Stowe, the author of *Uncle Tom's Cabin*. After two years of trial, it would end in a draw in July 1875, with Tilton destroyed, and Beecher tarnished, but not ejected from his lucrative church. Stanton and Anthony were also destroyed publicly because of their tight connection with Woodhull. It left the women's movement in absolute tatters and weakened by infighting. The effort for women's suffrage was stalled by the scandal; it would take another generation of women to see the Nineteenth Amendment ratified.

Upon her death, Elizabeth Cady Stanton's coffin rested on the mahogany Spirit Table. "At the head of her coffin was placed the mahogany McClintock Spirit Table, recalling the time when the woman's movement had begun."[47] Not included in the Smithsonian exhibit is any reference to the spirits. It was reliance upon the spirits that inspired the movement, but also the same reliance that destroyed it.

Eventually, spiritualism would die out, but the new trinity of feminism, free love, and occultism would continue, with the occult continuing as a consistent thread through the movement. Theosophy, Wicca, and other forms of pagan goddess worship continued to rise in popularity. Women saw it as their counter to the power of the patriarchy. It eventually became mainstream with popstars, following Madonna's lead, such as JLo, Beyoncé, Ariana Grande, and Halsey, decking themselves out as goddesses. They became the new poets with the kind of reach Percy Bysshe Shelley could only dream of, spreading the feminist messaging to billions of eager fans.

CHAPTER 4

Betty and the Communist Mystique

In the late 1980s, *Saturday Night Live* had a skit called "Unfrozen Caveman Lawyer." A caveman had been discovered frozen deep in a crevasse and thawed back to life again after one hundred thousand years. As a lawyer in the courtroom, the caveman was masterful. Tucked into an expensive suit, his heavy caveman unibrow, shaggy hair, and beard made it clear that he was still a caveman. He told the jurors his story and his experience of being overwhelmed by modern conveniences and afraid of modern man's ways. Cowed by the force of his simpleton arguments and appearance, the jurors overwhelmingly sided with his clients, no matter how ridiculous the case.

Betty Friedan is a bit like the caveman lawyer. *The Feminine Mystique*, published in 1963, was a runaway bestseller, selling nearly three million copies in its first three years of print. Her ideas were absorbed into the culture, even influencing millions of women who hadn't read it. Friedan always claimed that she hadn't paid any attention to women's issues until the 1950s and that she was just a normal, average housewife. But there was really nothing normal or average about this housewife.

A lot had changed in the feminist movement between the late 1890s and 1963, with quite a new cast of characters and ideologies at the helm. It was these new ideologies that animated Betty Friedan's *The Feminine Mystique*, which dramatically changed the way nearly every woman in America thought about her home, her life, her career, and her family.

After Stanton and Anthony

After the women's movement was largely rendered ineffective by division and scandals, a new generation of women moved into the roles once occupied by Elizabeth Cady Stanton and Susan B. Anthony. Some of those new leaders were the daughters of Stanton and her sisters in arms. World War I brought a renewed interest in women's suffrage after so many women went to work to support the war effort at home and abroad. On August 18, 1920, the Nineteenth Amendment was added to the Constitution. Women were given the right to vote.

After this period, the women's movement seemed to have lost its *cause célèbre*, and attention turned elsewhere. But despite appearances, the movement was being stoked and handled by a completely different set of leaders. No longer was it driven by women on a grassroots level, listening to spirits in their parlors at mahogany tables. A vast and more controlling network of powers was in charge. The messaging became Marxist, part of Soviet propaganda, a brackish mix of communist and feminist ideas. Communists generally saw the feminists as bourgeois, and the feminists saw the communists as much too narrow in their belief that women's issues sprang from the economy rather than culture. They had, however, a common goal in women's work. This goal and the overwhelming communist influence were enough that by the arrival of the second wave of feminism in the 1960s, the two had largely melded into one movement.

During this period, the tender relationship between mother and child begins to be erased from feminist rhetoric. There are no more testimonies like Mary Shelley's agony of missing her dear Wilmouse after his premature death, nor are there heartrending testimonies like Sojourner Truth's of losing her own thirteen children to slavery: "I have born thirteen children, and seen most of 'em sold into slavery, and when I cried out with my mother's grief, none but Jesus heard me—and ain't I a woman?"[1] Any discussion of what a mother's heart feels for a child drops off dramatically, with feminist rhetoric rife with the language of drudgery, burden, and exhaustion that afflict the lives of women with children. Tender memories like Mary Shelley's recollection of hair and giggles, wonder and joy, no longer have a place in the movement.

Communist Influence

Socialism had already been gaining a foothold when Karl Marx exploded onto the scene with his publications *The Communist Manifesto* (1848) and later *Capital* (1867).[2] Marx and his colleague Friedrich Engels seemed to add the fire that socialism had lacked, rallying comrades from around the world to fight for a communist utopia, where the poor would find justice and the oppressors would find a noose.

Marx believed that bourgeois culture was the enemy of the world, with the capitalists building comfortable lives upon the backs of poor, starving workers. The capitalists were the oppressors, the workers the oppressed. Marx believed in a glorious communist revolution where the workers would rise and destroy their oppressors once and for all. It was this ideology that underpinned the killing of the Russian tsar Nicholas II and his family, shot in their heads then dumped down a mine shaft in the middle of the night, to make way for the bloody Bolshevik Revolution. The Soviets killed an estimated twenty million people—many in the gulags and the purges in which political enemies of the Soviets, guilty or not, were rounded up and executed.[3] Some have speculated that the numbers are much higher due to lax record keeping by the Soviets. And that was just the Soviet Union—Marx's philosophy also fueled bloody "revolutions" in Cuba, Korea, Cambodia, Vietnam, and China.

The radical nature of communism stirred up friend and foe alike. Many in the United States feared the Marxist effort to infiltrate American institutions. The Red Scare, that the Soviets could take over America, was a real threat, but for most Americans, it didn't become a reality in their minds until the 1950 trial involving Whittaker Chambers and Alger Hiss. Hiss was a high-level federal employee, with a seemingly unimpeachable career: director of the Office of Special Political Affairs, executive secretary of the Dumbarton Oaks Conference (a conference on the formation of the United Nations), and later a delegate to the Yalta Conference at the end of World War II. All the while, as the trial revealed, Hiss had been sharing information with the Soviets and steering U.S. policies to be more in line with Soviet interests.

While Americans slept during the 1900s through the 1930s, figuratively and literally, the American Communist Party (ACP) and the Soviet Communist Party (SCP) worked in tandem and independently to infiltrate every aspect of American life and government. They worked quietly and discreetly, with no interest in notoriety or fortune, but only in the effort to promote communism. When the Depression hit in 1929, millions of Americans joined the Communist Party, which was already deeply entrenched in American institutions, believing capitalism was a failed effort after a cataclysmic stock market crash and wide economic collapse.

The Chambers-Hiss trial was provoked by Whittaker Chambers's defection from the Communist Party, where he had been an underground operative in the federal government. Chambers wrote eloquently about his conversion of heart away from materialist Marxism, prompted in many small ways but begun in part as he studied the tiny ear of his infant daughter:

> I was watching her eat. She was the most miraculous thing that had ever happened in my life. I liked to watch her even when she smeared porridge on her face or dropped it meditatively on the floor. My eye came to rest on the delicate convolutions of her ear—those intricate, perfect ears. The thought passed through my mind: "No, those ears were not created by any chance coming together of atoms in nature (the Communist view). They could have been created only by immense design."[4]

Chambers spent years planning his escape from the communist web in which he was embedded, knowing errors could result in his death or the deaths of family members. His planning, especially the files he took with Hiss's handwriting on them, would be the demise of Hiss and definite proof to all Americans that the communists were entrenched inside the U.S. government. Shortly thereafter, Julius Rosenberg and Ethel Rosenberg were convicted of "conspiracy to commit espionage" for the Soviets in 1951 and executed in 1953.

The Hiss trial and the execution of the Rosenbergs opened the floodgates of public knowledge about the communist threat to the United States. It also ushered in what many have called Senator Joseph McCarthy's witch hunt for communist infiltrators into the government, education, politics, and Hollywood. While McCarthy surfaced plenty of evidence exposing communist infiltrators in U.S. society, the net effect was one that ultimately freed communists from being silent about their Red allegiances. McCarthy's mishandling of the committee and feverish search for those who worked against American national security ended up making the Red Scare a "moral panic" in the historical record. The word "McCarthyism" became synonymous with a bad joke or a frenzied panic about boogeymen who didn't exist. McCarthy's efforts backfired, removing any real threat to those who engaged in communist activity.

Communist defectors, such as Whittaker Chambers and later Bella Dodd, attested to communism's cult-like effect on its adherents, serving as a kind of religion and not a benign one. Dodd explained that it became all-consuming in ways rivaled only by the experience of the saints and their great sacrifices for their faith. "Step by step," she wrote, "I retreated from God and went forth to meet the world, the flesh, and the devil.... I'd join the devil himself. There is no doubt that I traveled with him at my side and that he extorted a great price for his company."[5] Dodd would eventually extract herself from the party, but it too came with great reprisal, and damage to her name, career, and relationships, and even threats to her life. Dodd made clear that her experience of the Communist Party was that it took more than it could give, and it took nearly everything from her.

Congress of American Women

The Soviet Union and the way it treated women were considered by U.S. communists to be something of a "beacon on the hill" of what might be achieved in America. The Soviets, given the communist priority of work and political party over all else, viewed women through an androgynous lens, sending women out to work, corralling children in government care, and providing limitless abortions to ensure that work wasn't interrupted under the justification of liberation. Many of these ideals would make their way into American culture forty to fifty years later, and the Congress of American Women (CAW) was an important part of that effort.

This organization was set up legally by then party member Bella Dodd. Dodd wrote in her book, *School of Darkness*, about the reasons for establishing CAW:

> Late in 1945 word had come from Jessica Smith, wife of John Abt, who was in Moscow, that it was important that American women be organized into an international movement, ostensibly for peace. An international federation was to be established with Russian and French Party women as leaders. So during the next months I helped organize the United States branch. A combination of wealthy women and Party members established and maintained what was called the Congress of American Women.
>
> Since it was supposedly a movement for peace, it attracted many women. But it was really only a renewed offensive to control American women, a matter of deep importance to the communist movement, for American women do 80 per cent of the family spending. In the upper brackets they own a preponderance of capital stock and bonds. They are important in the making of political decisions. Like youth and minority groups, they are regarded as a reserve force of the revolution because they are more easily moved by emotional appeals. So the Soviet campaign for peace was especially geared to gain support of the women.[6]

Peace was the constant refrain heard around the world, particularly within the effort to "convert" women to the communist cause—intellectually, emotionally, and in their spending habits, a vital piece for the fight against capitalism. Other women's interests, such as childcare, equal rights, and defeating fascism, were among CAW conference topics.

The reverence for the Soviet system was evident at CAW meetings, where the Soviet delegates were treated like revered older sisters and the speeches were saturated with propaganda: "The Soviet Union is the only nation in the world where care for children constitutes one of the most important aspects of governmental and public activities, and where the State devotes special attention to the needs of the mother."[7] While this sounded nice in theory, what the Soviets were doing was stripping women of their motherhood through easy and free abortions that became a national type of birth control. Abortions became so common that eventually the party had to provide incentives for women to have children because their replacement birthrates were so low. If a woman chose to have a baby, the goal was to get her back to work as soon as possible, with the child's care placed in the hands of others. This all sounds rather pedestrian to us today as most of these practices have been absorbed by the West, but they were radical back in the early and mid-twentieth century.

The membership of CAW was a veritable who's who of communist—or communist-sympathizing—women, largely drawn from academia. Among them was Dorothy W. Douglas, a professor from Smith College who left her senator husband and became a lesbian, along with Susan B. Anthony II, the grandniece of the suffragette. Eleanor Flexner, later the author of *Century of Struggle*, a widely read history of the women's suffrage movement from a hidden communist perspective, was also a member.[8] As was Betty Friedan.

The CAW came under the microscope of the House Un-American Activities Committee in the U.S. House of Representatives in 1949, prior to the Chambers-Hiss trials. It was targeted as a Soviet front group and disbanded, though many of the members kept their Soviet connections and allegiances.

The Patriarchy

Communist ideology aimed to rouse the oppressed to overthrow their oppressors. This gave new currency to women as victims who must triumph over men. Not surprisingly, even the term "patriarchy," used in a negative sense, came from the communists. Friedrich Engels was first to use the language of the patriarchy, even though previous thinkers had already placed universal blame on the shoulders of men. It was Engels's usage that gave us the modern understanding of patriarchy as a male system of power used to control women.

Engels got the idea from a classicist named Johann Jakob Bachofen, whose 1861 book called *Das Mutterrecht* ("Mother Right") spoke of new anthropological studies about early matriarchies. Bachofen was fascinated by the Romantic idea, evident in the work of Percy Shelley, that men and women are opposites: men are light, law, order, and like God, while women are dark, earthy, creative, and like Satan. Bachofen didn't go so far as to endorse the view that women were like Satan, but called them "the bloody law of the earth," while men were "the pure celestial power of the sun."[9] These concepts were not entirely new, with similarities to Greek mythology, but what was new was the general association of men with God and women with the devil.

"Engels," then, as a journalist explained, "in The Origin of the Family, Private Property and the State, drew deeply on Bachofen in order to argue that patriarchy was a crucial factor in the emergence of capitalism."[10] The key issue that made the patriarchy problematic for Engels was its connection to fatherhood, monogamy, and, of course, private property, the last of which was much too capitalist an idea for him. The patriarchy, according to Engels, brought about "the world-historical defeat of the female sex. The man took command in the home also; the woman was degraded and reduced to servitude, she became the slave of his lust and a mere instrument for the production of children."[11] The father represented the bourgeoisie, while the mother and children were the proletariat. Engels's description of mothers as a "mere instrument for production of children" seems an odd description given the priority of production among all communists. Here Engels uses production condescendingly, as if it isn't important. But Engels's significant influence on the women's movement didn't end there.

What about Homemaking?

Another way in which communism crept into daily life was in the realm of homemaking. In the late 1800s, there were calls to end home-making altogether. In 1891 a woman named Lillie D. White wrote an article called "Housekeeping" in which she states: "Woman's work, her place, and sphere so entirely separated from man's special fields of action is a mumbo jumbo that has been revered too long and must be dethroned."[12] Another author, William Thompson, "saw the home as a 'prison-house of the wife,' an institution 'chiefly for the drillings of a superstition to render her more submissive.' The house, along with everything in it, was the husband's property, 'and of all fixtures the most abjectly his is his breeding machine, the wife.'"[13]

Neither Marx nor Engels discussed the question of homemaking, instead arguing that much of the women's movement was focused on petty bourgeois concerns. Homemaking came up in the United States when Mary Inman wrote about how housewives should unite as communists in her 1940 book, *In Woman's Defense.* Intense debate broke out among Communist Party members in the United States as to whether or not housewives actually produced anything and therefore were part of the essential caste of producers. Finally, much to Mary Inman's chagrin, party leaders decided that housewives did not produce anything and therefore that homemaking was no longer an acceptable form of communist work. "Party leaders criticized Inman's work," wrote Kate Weigand in her book *Red Feminism*, "not because she wanted to organize women but because they were worried that her equation of domestic work with productive labor glorified housework and could be used to reinforce the reactionary notion that women's place was in the home."[14] Homemaking in general should be discouraged, they agreed. Apparently, being a "mere instrument for the production of children," as Engels had said before, was not persuasive enough to fit homemaking into the category of real production. This final word put the nail in the homemakers' coffin across the Communist Party. With this proclamation, it was open season on homemaking for party members, and Betty Friedan picked up this notion and ran with it.

The Feminine Mystique

In 1963, Betty Friedan published *The Feminine Mystique*, presenting herself as a simple housewife with no career ambition and a newly formed sense of feminism. The reality was quite different. Daniel Horowitz and his wife, Helen, who were friends of Friedan's, suspected that there was more to her story after Helen noticed Friedan's use of communist community-organizing skills during her temporary professorship at the University of Southern California in the 1980s. These types of strategies, originally developed by radical activist Saul Alinsky, were not something an average housewife would happen to pick up; they were used by communists and other radicals of the New Left in the 1940s and beyond.

Horowitz started to dig a bit more and found a trove of useful information among Friedan's public papers: "I found papers Friedan had written in an undergraduate course on socialism and works, an FBI report concerning her alleged activity in the early 1940s, scores of articles in the labor press in the 1940s and 1950s signed by Betty Goldstein (Friedan's maiden name), and evidence of Friedan's participation in a rent strike in the early 1950s."[15] Slowly, the significance of these finds came together. "Though most women's historians have argued that 1960s feminism emerged in response to the suburban captivity of white middle class women during the 1950s, the material in Friedan's papers suggested additional origins—anti-fascism, radicalism, and labor union activism in the 1940s."[16]

Horowitz found enough evidence to approach Friedan about writing an authorized biography about her. He argued that McCarthyism had done so much damage to America that people such as Friedan, who were gifted communist activists, felt they had to hide their backgrounds for fear of reprisal. He wanted to correct that. Friedan bristled at the request, asserting that she hadn't known anything about feminism until the 1950s. She informed him that his argument was "innuendo," party-speak for incriminating information. She added that he would never be given access to her private papers for his stated purpose, and that if she discovered that he had, her lawyers would take care of the situation.

But Horowitz remained convinced that Friedan's story must be told. He wanted to expose the true damage of McCarthyism, and he believed people would see that Friedan was better than they already knew her to be because of her courageous communist background. Despite not having access to Friedan's private papers, Horowitz was still able to make a tight case.

Friedan had been born Bettye Goldstein (she would later drop the *e*) in 1921 in Peoria, Illinois, the daughter of Harry Goldstein and Miriam Horwitz Goldstein. She had a stormy relationship with her consistently unhappy mother, who was disappointed in her daughter's large nose and argued that Betty worked at being ugly. Friedan believed that her mother's unhappiness was because she was home and unable to work at her husband's jewelry store.[17] Later, she attributed her own interest in feminism to her mother's discontent.

Betty was an excellent student and writer and went on to Smith College, where she was active with the student paper. But she was also volatile, and even at times violent, traits that would follow her into adulthood.[18] At Smith, she came under the wing of Dorothy W. Douglas, former wife of a senator and a lesbian, who mentored her in the thought of Marx. She wrote of her new radicalism in the college paper, and in her "senior year everything came together—passionately advocating anti-fascism, unionization, equality for women and progressive psychology," a new branch of psychology that embraced leftist concepts.[19] After she graduated from Smith, she went on to graduate school at the University of California, Berkeley, and ended up working as a journalist for Federated Press and later for the UE labor union, known then as "the largest Communist-led institution of any kind in the United States."[20]

Up to this point, there was very little about her life that was not somehow intertwined with communist or progressive politics, including a boyfriend who was a member of the Communist Party and who worked with Robert Oppenheimer, the scientist who developed the atom bomb.[21] In one of her first jobs as a journalist for the Federated Press, Betty reviewed the book *Why Women Cry*, writing, "Men, there's a revolution cooking in your own kitchens—revolutions of the forgotten female, who is finally waking up to the fact that she can produce other things besides babies."[22] This suggests that she became interested in feminist ideas long before she claimed.

Friedan, like many radicals of her time, was focused on fighting fascism. Hitler's brand of fascism included the slogan *Kinder, Küche, Kirche*, or "children, kitchen, church." For Friedan and others, these were the elements to fight, believing adherence to children, kitchen, and church was the engine for Hitler's fascism, instead of merely window dressing. Friedan saw communism as the opposite side of Hitler's repressive coin. Like others of her day, she overlooked the inconvenient details about Joseph Stalin's collusion with Hitler and the deep connections between the deadly tyrannies of Hitler and Stalin.

In 1947, Betty married Carl Friedan and was eventually fired from her work because she was pregnant. They moved from an urban borough of New York out to an old mansion on the Hudson River, where she wrote *The Feminine Mystique*. The idea, she said, was sparked by a survey she sent to her fellow Smith alumnae about their happiness at home as wives and mothers. The responses told her that she was not alone in her feeling of boredom and discontent. Or, at least, that was the story she told about the book's origin. A closer look reveals its deeper communist influences.

In chapter 9, "The Sexual Sell," Friedan writes: "Some months ago, as I began to fit together the puzzle of women's retreat to home, I had the feeling I was missing something." She continues:

> Why is it never said that the really crucial function, the really important role that women serve as housewives is to *buy more things for the house*. In all the talk of femininity and woman's role, one forgets that the real business of America is business. But the perpetuation of housewifery, the growth of the feminine mystique, makes sense (and dollars) when one realizes that women are the chief customers of American business. Somehow, somewhere, someone must have figured out that women will buy more things if they are kept in the underused, nameless-yearning, energy-to-get-rid-of state of being housewives.[23]

Here is where it gets really interesting:

> I suddenly realized the significance of the boast that women wield seventy-five per cent of the purchasing power in America. I suddenly saw American women as *victims* of that ghastly gift, that power at the point of purchase.[24]

This is perhaps the most interesting and revealing passage, exposing her communist slip. She starts the argument as if just mentioning something that she off-handedly discovered, perhaps while thinking about it at the checkout at the grocery store, or maybe it came to her while peeling potatoes, but the details of it look very similar to the description offered by Bella Dodd for the reasons why CAW was established:

> But it was really only a renewed offensive to control American women, a matter of deep importance to the communist movement, for American women do 80 per cent of the family spending. In the upper brackets they own a preponderance of capital stock and bonds. They are important in the making of political decisions.... So the Soviet campaign for peace was especially geared to gain support of the women.[25]

The percentages of women's purchasing power have been changed slightly, but the general message is the same: women are spending too much money, which is holding up the capitalist model that communism wants to eradicate. This is not the feminist talking point of a naïve housewife, but rather comes straight from the Congress of American Women.

Meanwhile, Horowitz also found a paragraph from Engels written in one of Friedan's journals.

> We see already that the emancipation of women and their
> equality with men are impossible and must remain so as
> long as women are excluded from socially productive work
> and restricted to housework, which is private. The emanci-
> pation of women becomes possible only when women are
> enabled to take part in production on a large, social scale,
> and when domestic duties require their attention only to a
> minor degree.[26]

The main point here, echoing Marx and Engels's model of motherhood, was that women would only truly be free when they entered the
paid work force. She saw that women wouldn't do it voluntarily but
needed coaxing and a good heave to be pushed out of their homes.[27] In
The Feminine Mystique, she was able to play up the dissatisfying
aspects of being at home with children without ever speaking of the
positives. Her original audience, fellow Smith alumnae, like many
women today, had spent most of their lives doing things unrelated to
homemaking, so when it was time to do it, few were adept at many of
its required duties. These elements were enough to stir up dissatisfaction
in many women, creating a kind of contagion. There was nothing
nuanced about her rhetoric regarding homemaking. In *The Feminine
Mystique*, she wrote, "Perhaps it is only a sick or immature society that
chooses to make women 'housewives,' not people. Perhaps it is only
sick or immature men and women, unwilling to face the great challenges of society, who can retreat for long, without unbearable distress,
into that thing-ridden house and make it the end of life itself."[28]

Friedan goes so far as to compare homemaking with "a comfortable concentration camp."[29] It is hard to wrap one's head around how
overwrought this comparison is. What the starved, gassed, lice-infested,
raped, brutalized, tortured, and ultimately exterminated people in
the real concentration camps would have given to live like the most

privileged women in human history. This comparison reveals how eager Friedan was to make women at home dissatisfied with their lot.

Using psychology and consciousness-raising tactics, Friedan convinced American women that they would be happier if they left their homes and got paying work, for she believed, truly, work will set us free. Her book was animated by the same ideology used by Hitler—*Arbeit Macht Frei*—a motto blazoned on the gates of Auschwitz. She knew that just telling women that they should abandon their homes to realize the Marxist goal of putting women into the work force would fall upon deaf ears. Women needed to be convinced that staying home was a bad thing.

In 1975, the more strident Simone de Beauvoir, in an interview with Friedan, took this argument a step further: "No woman should be authorized to stay at home and raise her children. Society should be different. Women should not have that choice, precisely because if there is such a choice, too many women will make that one."[30] Both Friedan and de Beauvoir knew that their effort to remove women from home was a fragile one that required plenty of rhetoric to stick, because few women wanted to leave their homes.

Friedan's enterprise never was just the work of your average housewife in a "comfortable concentration camp." The complaints of *The Feminine Mystique* were not really hers, but were the practiced grievances of a longstanding political movement. Even her husband, Carl, agreed: "She had time to write it because she lived in a mansion on the Hudson River, had a full-time maid and was completely supported by me."[31] The couple later divorced.

Friedan's ideas became enshrined in the women's movement, especially with her role in establishing the National Organization for Women (NOW), which provided significant political heft behind the abortion debate, the Equal Rights Amendment (ERA), and the later inclusion of LGBT+ rights into the movement. During her lifetime, she saw her efforts rewarded with a massive societal shift away from the home and toward the Soviet model celebrated by the Congress of American Women.

Although Friedan never acknowledged her communist roots, plenty of later feminists unabashedly proclaimed their intellectual allegiances, including Shulamith Firestone, Kate Millett (often called the "Female Marx"[32]), and Angela Davis. Feminism had become just another aspect of American life infiltrated by the communists, now promoting their ideals, their vision, and their plan for women.

CHAPTER 5

Kate and the Lost Girls' Triumph

In the late 1960s, somewhere in the west Greenwich Village section of New York City, at Lila Karp's apartment, twelve women, led by Kate Millett, sat around a large table and repeated this chant: "Why are we here today?" the chairwoman asked.

"To make revolution."
"What kind of revolution?"
"The Cultural Revolution."
"And how do we make Cultural Revolution?"
"By destroying the American family!"
"How do we destroy the family?"
"By destroying the American Patriarch."
"And how do we destroy the American Patriarch?"
"By taking away his power!"
"How do we do that?"

"By destroying monogamy!"

"How can we destroy monogamy?"

"By promoting promiscuity, eroticism, prostitution, abortion, and homosexuality!"[1]

Read the last line again. These practices were not part of American culture at that time, but all of them have been achieved today, probably beyond the wildest dreams of those at that meeting.

Kate Millett (1934–2017) was a keen agent in the sexual revolution. The author of *Sexual Politics*, she was known as the "Female Marx," and later "the high priestess of feminism."[2] What Millett did was what so many women before her had only attempted: she devised a way to utterly destroy the patriarchy. Mallory Millett, Kate's sister, has told the story of the tony, upper class women Kate brought together in New York City in the late 1960s and early '70s. These women, building on earlier feminist and communist ideas, laid the groundwork for and executed the ideas of second-wave feminism.

In the 1960s and '70s, the whole world was in a vast upheaval. Vietnam, Woodstock, psychedelic drugs, universal consciousness, the civil rights movement, the Pill, a string of political assassinations, the Second Vatican Council, the Cold War, the nuclear threat—the culture was rocked by change and transformation. Fear of reprisal from the Red Scare seemed to be on its way out, and any fear that Betty Friedan had felt about her communist links was not shared by feminists such as Kate Millett, Angela Davis, or Shulamith Firestone.

The sexual revolution was in full swing, and the second wave of feminism was like gasoline on its early flames. It was aided significantly by the popular work of Sigmund Freud (1856–1939) and Alfred Kinsey (1894–1956), which reduced all people (including children and babies) to sexual beings motivated by sexual desire. Freud focused on our unconscious desires, while Kinsey, considered the first sexologist, found no sexual topic too taboo to investigate. The free love ideal that de Sade and Percy Shelley dreamed about became a reality.

Kate Millett was an intellectual force and the first American woman to be awarded first-class honors at Oxford in the 1950s, finishing her three-year program in just two years. She then went on to Columbia University, where she was mentored by philosopher and political theorist Herbert Marcuse of the Frankfurt School. Millett, who had already spent several years as a lesbian, living for two years at Oxford with her American lover, and inspired by the work of the eighteenth-century Marquis de Sade, was keen on smashing taboos. Marcuse helped fuel and direct her iconoclastic approach which resulted in her 1970s book *Sexual Politics*. Marcuse was to Millett what Marx and Engels had been to Friedan.

Herbert Marcuse (1898–1979) is known as the father of the New Left, a broad ranging socialist movement focused on social action. He is also one of the fathers of critical theory, which is the source of critical race theory and the woke ideology that developed later, which believed that societal structures, not individuals, were the reason for social problems. The structure of the traditional American society, for Marcuse, particularly sexual mores such as monogamy, were enslaving. These taboos needed to be torn down to make way for authentic freedom and happiness and to end the oppression of bourgeois society.

Marcuse used his platform as a professor to speak frequently to student groups, radicalizing them for the New Left. Like Kate Millett, he attracted and mentored nonconforming outsiders, like Angela Davis, and encouraged the artsy bohemian ethos on college campuses, driven by his sense that art can shift the culture. "Art cannot change the world," offered Marcuse, "but it can contribute to changing the consciousness and drives of the men and women who could change the world."[3] Using these tactics, Marcuse interjected Marx and Freud deep into the academy through his intellectual children, such as Millett, but also into hip culture. Marxism and the New Left were no longer just for intellectuals, but took on the vitally important "cool" factor.

Wilhelm Reich (1897–1957), another member of the Frankfurt School, coined the term "The Sexual Revolution" in a book of the same name.[4] Reich influenced feminist thought by his association with Simone de Beauvoir and Betty Friedan, as the sexual revolution he predicted in the 1930s became a reality several decades later. Millett was a close disciple of Wilhelm Reich, who had spoken of "sex politics" decades before that figured into her own later book *Sexual Politics*.

In his 1936 book, *The Sexual Revolution*, the Austrian-born doctor and psychoanalyst argued, like Engels before him, that the family was the problem. But Reich saw that the family could be reworked as an asset for the communist revolution. The key to this project was sexual freedom, particularly among children. "Sexual suppression produces a subordinate individual who simultaneously exhibits slavish obedience and rebellion,"[5] Reich asserted. True freedom, as William Godwin and de Sade had argued, is found in total sexual freedom.

A family's commitment to political radicalism could be gauged by how much it went against traditional mores; the more a family embraced free love and sexual freedom, the more it could be counted on to work for the revolution. "While asserting that the patriarchal family is the single most important unit of ideological control for an oppressive and totalitarian regime," writer Carl Trueman explains, "Reich also believes that the state must be used to coerce families and, where necessary, actively punish those who dissent from the sexual liberation being proposed."[6] For Reich the family had intrinsic power, which can be used either for totalitarian regimes, as in the case of the fascists, or for communism. (Of course, communist regimes are also totalitarian, but leaving that detail out was part of communist propaganda.) The defining characteristic of any family was how sexually liberated its members were.

While we often think of the sexual revolution as being the result of a confluence of factors, it was well laid out in Reich's work far in advance, and executed by people like Millett, de Beauvoir, and Angela Davis. The free love movement, wrapped in Freudian psychology and Marxist philosophy, aimed to destroy the traditional family. Reich was keen on trying to take power away from that most basic cell of society and give it to the state. Once the government had control over the family, it would have ultimate power over society. Reich went so far as to say that the government had an obligation to persecute those who would not engage in or encourage the sexual liberation of every member of the family.[7] Today, we are witnessing the effects of this philosophy with the advent of "drag queen story hour" in kindergartens and the aggressive sexual education of small children by disciples of Reich, Freud, Kinsey, and Millett that have been woven into popular and woke culture.

Millett offered the academic justification for feminism that became the backbone of women's studies programs nationally and was featured on *TIME* magazine's cover.[8] Her determination to bring down the patriarchy knew no bounds, nor did her wild lifestyle.

Millett was a huge advocate for abortion on demand. She watched as the young men fighting the communists in Vietnam were nationally criticized for killing innocent civilians. Rather than balking at the killing of innocents, she decided that women, too, had to have the courage to kill—not civilians in a combat zone, but their own children in their own wombs. This was her vision of equality. In her view, having an abortion became something of a badge of honor, long before women today made the same argument. Abortion was the primary way to equalize women and men because women were no longer saddled with an unwanted child and the years of dedication motherhood requires to raise that child.[9]

In her book *Sexual Politics*, Millett describes the patriarchy as an expansive ideology that leaves nothing untouched. The patriarchy, as Millett saw it, is the "most pervasive ideology of our culture and provides its most fundamental concept of power."[10] Patriarchy was inescapable in society's current configuration; every institution and all social norms were set up to manipulate and enslave women. Even romantic love "was simply a means of emotionally manipulating the female by the male, tricking her into subservience," wrote Charlotte Higgins. "Women were socialised into pleasing, flattering, entertaining and gratifying men."[11]

Kate saw that "patriarchy's chief institution is the family," so her solution was to dismantle the family in much the same way that the Soviet Union had done decades before.[12] "The Soviet Union," she explained, "did make a conscious effort to terminate patriarchy and restructure its most basic institution—the family. After the revolution every possible law was passed to free individuals from the claims of the family: free marriage and divorce, contraception, and abortion on demand. Most material of all, the women and children were to be liberated from the controlling economic power of the husband."[13] Kate's vision was merely a reiteration of the earlier efforts by the Soviets to dissolve the family because the family was viewed as the place where men were able to control their dependents.

In an effort to free themselves from men, Millett and others put lesbianism on a high pedestal. The Wonder Woman story that started in the 1940s came to life in the '70s with the television series featuring curvy Lynda Carter. Wonder Woman was a powerful and righteous superhero. Though not overtly a lesbian, she showed young girls how women could live in perfect harmony without men at her home of Paradise Island. She brought harmony to the rest of the world after the men messed it up.

Feminists began to argue in favor of the advantages of a lesbian lifestyle. "The Lesbian, through her ability to obtain love and sexual satisfaction from other women, is freed of dependence on men for love, sex, and money," it is explained in *Sisterhood is Powerful*. "She does not have to do menial chores for them (at least at home), nor cater to their egos, nor submit to hasty and inept sexual encounters. She is freed from fear of unwanted pregnancy and the pains of childbirth, and from the drudgery of child raising."[14]

One of the main goals of many of the second-wave feminists was to erase gender differences altogether. "Just as the end goal of socialist revolution was not only the elimination of the economic class *privilege* but of the economic class *distinction* itself," Shulamith Firestone, another Reich disciple, explained, "so the end goal of feminist revolution must be, unlike that of the first feminist movement, not just the elimination of male *privilege* but of the sex *distinction* itself: genital differences between human beings would no longer matter culturally."[15]

What Millett and her comrades put forward for American women truly was the embodiment of Shelley's mythological Cythna, the feminist ideal—a woman totally unconnected to relationships with husband and children, detached from the home, and sexually available, thanks to the Pill, to men and women alike, with few obvious long-term consequences.

Occult, Anyone?

Another key element that arose during the second wave was the occult. Like spiritualism and theosophy during Elizabeth Cady Stanton's time, this brand of the occult was more brazen and directed at women's angst toward men. Historically, witchcraft was used as a source of power for women, particularly those on the edge of society. It rose in popularity in the 1960s and '70s and found a permanent home in pop culture. Wiccan groups cropped up all over the country, including the WITCH covens, which stood for Women's International Terrorist Conspiracy from Hell: "WITCH is an all-women Everything.

It's theatre, revolution, magic, terror, joy, garlic flowers, spells. It's an awareness that witches and gypsies were the original guerrillas and resistance fighters against oppression—particularly the oppression of women—down through the ages."[16] Said to have been "born" on Halloween 1968, WITCH was featured in the 1970s book *Sisterhood is Powerful.* Their entry included a number of spells and hexes for everyday use.

On the West Coast in the early 1970s, Phyllis Chesler speaks of her friend "Z," short for Zsuzsanna, who formed a coven named for Susan B. Anthony in Santa Monica, California. It was "the first feminist, women-only Wiccan coven. Z may have single-handedly introduced pagan spirituality and goddess-centered religion in America." Z published several books, such as *The Feminist Book of Lights and Shadows* and *The Grandmother of Time: A Woman's Book of Celebrations, Spells, and Sacred Objects for Every Month of the Year.*[17]

Even the inaugural cover of *Ms.* magazine couldn't resist engaging in a little goddess worship, featuring an image of the Hindu goddess, Kali, juggling the demands of home and life with her many arms, while pregnant. The goddess, still worshipped by Hindus, is said to be sated by the death of men and animals, with her arms holding decapitated heads.

The examples of witchcraft and Wicca among prominent feminists were and remain legion. Horoscopes, psychics, use of tarot cards, and goddess and pagan worship continue to be popular. Many feminists speak whimsically about "the goddess within" and other sorts of pop paganism.

All Is Not Well

Over the years, the real stories of the second-wave feminist leaders have seeped out. For years, Millett was in and out of mental hospitals. She published books about her mental illness. She was known for not sleeping for days on end, giving talks that were supposed to be on feminism but turned into ceaseless tirades about the Irish "Troubles"—the thirty years of warring between Irish Catholics and the Northern Ireland Protestants. She was known for trying to sleep with just about everyone, including her own sister, which marked the end of their relationship. No topic was taboo, including her arguments in favor of pedophilia. Years later, she went on *Geraldo* to talk about mental illness, but denied having experienced it herself.[18]

In her 2018 book *A Politically Incorrect Feminist: Creating a Movement with Bitches, Lunatics, Dykes, Prodigies, Warriors, and Wonder Women*, one of the grandmothers of feminism, Phyllis Chesler, confirmed Kate's long history of mental illness and aggressive sexual behavior:

> Kate had a shitload of charm and, in the beginning, a commanding presence, but she also had periods in which she didn't sleep, raged at others, attempted suicide, and exploited her groupies—all the while feeling victimized by them (which she was). She couldn't be counted on to remain lucid at a press conference. She also fell in love, and tried to have her way, quite aggressively, with woman after woman (including me).[19]

Chesler describes Kate's unique mental illness, but she doesn't hold back from talking about other second-wave feminists and their "issues" as well. She reveals stories that have been jealously guarded by feminists for decades, particularly the fact that most of the women in the movement were incredibly broken by mental illness, sexual abuse, and drug abuse. Chesler calls them "the lost girls."[20]

For Millett, Chesler, and this early group of second-wavers, sisterhood was everything. Most had renounced men and were not just living in, but also idolizing lesbian relationships as the pinnacle of all relationships.[21] Their brokenness wasn't considered a weakness, but rather the glue that held them together. "We—who only yesterday had been viewed as cunts, whores, dykes, bitches, witches, and mad-women," Chesler explained, "we who had been second- and third-class citizens—had suddenly become players in history. The world would never be the same, and neither would we."[22]

Gloria Steinem was among them. Her father was a traveling salesman and left her as a child to take care of her mentally ill and bedridden mother for seven years, hardly a job for a child. Chesler herself had a critical and abusive mother, who, like Mary Wollstonecraft's mother, preferred her sons. "My parents were good nineteenth-century parents," Chesler explained. "I wanted for nothing—except affection, under-standing, the most minimal kindness, and privacy. I left home because my mother was cruel and hostile toward me and my father never inter-vened."[23] Shulamith Firestone had an overbearing father (who had sur-vived a concentration camp) and a passive mother. At various stages in their relationship, both father and daughter threatened to kill each other when Firestone was a child. She was a strong Marxist, declaring that pregnancy was barbaric and that women shouldn't be saddled with raising children. As a young woman, she descended into mental illness after her brother committed suicide.[24]

Andrea Dworkin was another "lost girl" feminist activist, who had a socialist father and a strained relationship with her mother. Andrea was molested by a stranger at the age of nine, and she claimed to have been abducted by aliens at twelve.[25] She was a prolific author, writing in novels and nonfictions books mainly about male sexual violence.

Perhaps the most "lost girl" of them all was Valerie Solanas, who wrote the manifesto for the Society for Cutting Up Men (SCUM):

> Life in this society being, at best an utter bore and no aspect
> of society being at all relevant to women, there remains to

civic-minded, responsible, thrill-seeking females only to overthrow the government, eliminate the money system, institute
complete automation, and destroy the male sex.[26]

Solanas offered an appealing future for the men that SCUM allowed
to exist: "The few remaining men can exist out their puny days dropped
out on drugs or strutting around in drag or passively watching the
high-powered female in action, fulfilling themselves as spectators,
vicarious livers or breeding in the cow pasture with the toadies, or they
can go off to the nearest friendly neighborhood suicide center where
they will be quietly, quickly, and painlessly gassed to death."[27] Chesler
describes the SCUM Manifesto, written around 1966, as "an angry,
frightening, kick-ass feminist work. It's daring and brilliant, a clarion
call to arms, perhaps satiric, probably literal." And sadly, there were
tragic reasons for Solanas's mental illness:

> [She] was a physically abused child and incest victim who
> became homeless at fifteen; she was a lesbian, a panhandler,
> and a prostitute. Solanas gave birth to a child when she
> was seventeen; the child was taken from her. Solanas's life
> history resembles that of Aileen Wuornos, the woman who
> became known as the "first female serial killer" and the
> "hitchhiking prostitute."[28]

Not surprisingly, "Solanas became known as the woman who tried
to kill Andy Warhol," Chesler explains unflinchingly. "In her mind
Warhol had promised to film her play, 'Up Your Ass,' which is about a
prostitute who kills a man. Warhol never made the film; in Solanas's
mind he had ruined her career."[29] So she shot him. He survived but had
irreparable damage to his organs. Solanas later died alone in a hotel in
California. Solanas's vitriol did not die with her. Echoes of it are found

regularly in feminist writings and social media posts. HuffPost editor
Emily McCombs repeated the idea in 2022: "New Year's resolutions:
1. Cultivate female friendships 2. Band together to kill all men."[30]

These "lost girls" crafted a new society based upon "the sisterhood," the relationship between women. But the sisterhood meant so
much more than just sisters—it meant lovers as well. Some of them were
married to men at different points. Millett, who was a lesbian in college
and graduate school, was married to a man for several years, but then
returned to a lesbian lifestyle, later marrying a woman when it became
legal. Dworkin was married twice. Her first marriage quickly ended,
with Dworkin leaving her husband because of the terrible abuse she
endured at his hands. Her second marriage was a long-term and open
relationship in which both Dworkin and her husband also took same-sex
partners. Chesler was married to men twice, but also later came out as
a lesbian. Steinem was married for three years to David Bale, father of
Christian Bale, until he passed away in 2003, but never had children of
her own. She later spoke of being attracted to both men and women.[31]

There were also limits to the sisterhood. As with any family, there
was drama. Chesler shed light on the infighting, the jealousies, the
intellectual theft, and the jockeying for attention with which these
women afflicted each other. For all the promises of the sisterhood,
their relationships had the same vices as relationships with men. Phyllis
Chesler speaks in her book about how she couldn't figure out why her
lesbian partners weren't that into her son and abandoned him after their
relationships ended.[32] Shulamith Firestone died alone in her apartment
with no one to care for her. Her body was found a week after her death;
she is thought to have died of starvation.

Nearly every one of these women was affected by one or several
major struggles in her life, including mental health issues, mother
wounds, father wounds, sexual abuse, abortions, suicides, drug over-
doses, bipolar disorders, depression, and run-ins with the law. These

elements drew these women together, sustaining their anger and passion to fight the system. But these women, these lost girls, also set the cultural agenda according to which we live today. These are the women who told us to hate the patriarchy and view men as the true enemies of womankind, who told us that "choice" was better than life, convincing us that our children were an obstacle to our happiness, that the vulnerability that comes with giving life was the real enemy.

Lost Girls Make More Lost Girls

In 1973, the Supreme Court in *Roe v. Wade* invented a constitutional right to abortion and legalized abortion across the United States, undoing existing state laws protecting unborn children. Overnight, abortion, essentially for any reason and at any stage of pregnancy, became the law of the land. This was something for which the second-wave feminists fought. It was also something that Hugh Hefner advocated for years before it would become law. Hefner, the founder of *Playboy* magazine, saw the benefits for men everywhere. If a baby could be "taken care of," the demands of paternity would simply melt away.

But the effects of abortion on women were devastating, and it required plenty of rhetoric and marketing to keep women from seeing that the babies they were aborting were their own children. Euphemisms were employed by feminists, such as "clump of cells" and "product of conception." The madness, sadness, and brokenness of the lost girls was passed along to other women.

Rock sensation Stevie Nicks offered a rare glimpse into her life in the 1990s. It was a bizarre look at a woman who had lived by the work-over-family creed, intoxicated by fame, money, and drugs. The interview addresses Nicks's pain connected to her own success, while also offering a glimpse into the odd childishness she embodies as a grown and successful woman:

Stevie points out her favourite chaise lounge. Her favourite doll, which resembles her, sits regally upon it. One, a favourite 12-year-old garment, is loosely draped around the chanteuse. Stevie needs the comfort of long-familiar possessions: they stress a continuity and equilibrium that have been sadly lacking in her emotional life.[33]

She speaks of the men in her life and the abortions she had:

"They are all very smart and very loving, and they all had a difficult time with my life and the way that I live it and how busy I am." For four lovers, a crucial test came when she became pregnant and opted for terminations. "It's always been a tragedy. But they understood." But they didn't really. "Eventually, their hearts couldn't take it, they couldn't understand quite enough, how deeply embedded in this I was. And so it eventually hurt them too much and they had to leave, or face devastation on their own."[34]

Nicks is open about the damage she incurred from the demands of her work and the abortions it resulted in:

But now there is remorse at the havoc her abortions have wreaked on her psyche. "To give up four (babies) is to give up a lot that would be here now. So that really bothers me, a lot, and really breaks my heart. But they're gone, so . . ." she composes herself. "But I couldn't because I was too busy. And I had all these commitments."[35]

Today, broken celebrities are a dime a dozen. Their stories have made us callous to the idea that an abortion is awful; today, we are meant to see an abortion as badge of honor. In 2015, a viral social media post launched an ongoing campaign, featured in Oprah Winfrey's *O* magazine, urging women to "shout" their abortions. Celebrities such as Michelle Williams, Jennifer Grey, Alyssa Milano, Uma Thurman, Chelsea Handler, and Lil' Kim spoke pridefully of how their abortions had made their careers possible.[36]

More than a career-maker, abortion has been made into a kind of rite of passage by actress and director Lena Dunham, among other women. Dunham's latest television series featured the first "abortion baby shower." We can see the influence of the lost girls on the young woman who said this on TikTok:

> If I ever have to have an abortion, you bet I'm gonna have an
> [expletive] party. I'm like gonna have like cupcakes with like
> aborted fetuses drawn on them. Lots of snacks, lots—I'm
> gonna come up with some sort of cocktail and call it the
> "aborted fetus." And me and all of my friends are just gonna
> hang out, eat a bunch of yummy dead-fetus-themed food, get
> drunk, and have a great old time.[37]

The gradual transition of rhetoric on abortion is startling. What was supposed to be "safe, legal, and rare" gradually turned into something to gloat about, with each generation since *Roe*'s arrival becoming more disconnected from the reality of who it is that is being aborted—their own children—and what it should mean to us as women.

The Triumph

After reading about these broken women, it is easy to see why many believe that feminism took a sharp turn in the 1960s and '70s. But the ideas underpinning their work were already extant. They were embodied in new and startling ways in the "new" and improved version of the 1870s trinity—feminism, free love, and the occult. The 1970s version of feminism was built on the same ideas, only on steroids this time. Millett, her followers, and the other grandmothers of second-wave feminism set the diabolical narrative that has affected nearly every woman on the planet. These broken women are responsible for the fifty-year-old claim that female empowerment can only be achieved through promiscuity, abortion, and the destruction of the family.

The ideas of previous feminists came home to roost: Mary Wollstonecraft's idea about women as human beings and the hollowing out of womanhood. William Godwin's dream of getting rid of the shackles of the family and replacing them with free love. Percy Shelley's vision of Cythna, a woman who wasn't a wife or mother. Elizabeth Stanton's openness to the occult and the supplanting of the Christian myth with a different kind of Eve, wise and not in need of a Savior. And finally, Friedan's communist effort to save the world by getting women to work. With all of these behind her, Kate articulated how to best destroy the patriarchy, with her litany and her push to end every taboo. But what Kate and all the others missed was that these efforts weren't just harming men, they were harming everyone touched by their ideologies.

Part II

The Mean Girls

The 1980s ushered in a new phase of feminism, during which the radical ideas of the 1960s and '70s took deep root in the culture. While certainly there were and have always been "mean girls," these next two chapters will look more specifically at the tactics used by feminists and even their male friends, such as Hugh Hefner and Phil Donahue, that gave radical feminism such a hold on American women's minds. Mean girls, or mean girl tactics, are those used to hide data, mislead, or outright lie about information that might hurt the feminist movement. Mean girls frequently employ smiles and/or euphemisms as part of the deception to avoid betraying their devious actions.

The mean girls from the 1980s up to the present have influenced how hundreds of millions of women would come to think about themselves, their bodies, their work, their families, their husbands, and their children. Using lots of advertising dollars on television and radio, they bulldozed their way through the culture wars with pithy phrases: *Smash the Patriarchy*; *Pro-Choice*; *My Body, My Choice*; Planned Parenthood, and so on. Female equality, for the mean girls, morphed into power to influence through their celebrity status, to sway the culture, and to line their own pockets.

There are manifold reasons why the mean girls have emerged, but it is partly because feminism proposes to fix women's problems without having the right solution. Feminism started with the wrong question, and it led to the wrong solution. Feminism has had to rely on power, manipulation, and control to enforce and extend its influence.

Feminism offered us women's studies and women's health and women's rights, but they didn't tell anyone, even once solid data was in, that their goals leave women miserable, unhealthy, and wondering what we did wrong. They didn't tell us that the life they want us to live serves those in power, not us. Their goal via the sexual revolution was to reject motherhood, monogamy, and marriage in favor of hookups, money, glamour, and it has left so many unfulfilled, and deeply unhappy. The mean girls are more powerful when we are enslaved, broken, dependent, and alone, because then we need them more. We need their magazines, their health fixes, their counseling, their diets, their experts, their advice, and they take our outpouring of cash all the way to the bank.

The mean girls can be found among the elite women in every sphere of culture: politics, academics, fashion, magazines, publishing, Hollywood. These women and their male allies promoted the crooked feminist narrative, unwittingly transforming so many of us into promiscuous pagans, using any means necessary, under the guise of "independent thinking."

The mean girls of these chapters disseminated the narrative and then cemented it into the culture. Like dictates in the movie *Mean Girls*—"On Wednesdays, we wear pink"—American women have been served a set of instructions that came down from our cultural "betters."

There is no doubt that there are mean boys, but there is something unique about the actions taken by the mean girls. These actions are often hidden, two-faced, and frequently performed with a smile, with those on the receiving end scratching their heads about what is really happening.

CHAPTER 6

Gloria and Selling Feminism

The feminist movement has been incredibly successful. There are a lot of reasons for its success, but much of it has to do with crafting and controlling a message that has resonated with women for five decades now. Gloria Steinem has been at the heart of much of it. *Ms.* magazine, cofounded by Steinem, splashed out into the world in the 1970s and was unlike any other magazine. It was savvy, edgy, irreverent, and boundary breaking. It showed the world and women exactly what the editors wanted them to see. It became a feminist icon—a solid brand for the feminist movement.

While *Ms.* magazine felt new, the concept of public relations was not. Public relations and marketing have become so commonplace in the world today that we scarcely notice their underlying buzz. But at some point, it was new. The father of public relations is Edward Bernays, the double nephew—on both his father's and mother's side—of Sigmund Freud. Using his uncle's work, Bernays saw that appealing to people's

emotions is the key to successful propaganda. For Bernays, propaganda was an important new way of organizing democracy around the
inherent chaos of modernity, especially as news spread faster and faster.

"The conscious and intelligent manipulation of the organized
habits and opinions of the masses is an important element in democratic society," Bernays explained. "Those who manipulate this unseen
mechanism of society constitute an invisible government which is the
true ruling power of our country."[1] In his 1928 book *Propaganda*,
Bernays explained its effectiveness: "By playing upon an old cliché,
or manipulating a new one, the propagandist can sometimes swing
a whole mass of group emotions."[2] The key for Bernays, as it was for
his famous uncle, and so many who came after them, was to drill into
the emotions, the unconscious—not reason, not logic, and not truth.

Bernays believed his type of propaganda was particularly useful
for women, as witnessed with the suffrage movement. "If I seemed to
concentrate on the accomplishments of women in politics, it is because
they afford a particularly striking example of intelligent use of the new
propaganda to secure attention and acceptance of minority ideas."[3]
Through propaganda, minority ideas can easily sway a majority when
the right combination of messaging is communicated.

Bernays's most dramatic work as a propagandist was in 1929 when
he was hired to help get women smoking. The American Tobacco
Company realized that if they could get the other half of the population hooked on smoking, profits would go through the roof. "It will
be like opening a gold mine right in our front yard," said the tobacco
executive who hired Bernays. Bernays's idea was to stage a photoshoot
during the Easter parade in New York. He told the attractive but not
too "model-y" women that their cigarettes represented freedom for
women. Cigarettes were to become "Torches of Freedom" signaling
that all liberated women smoked, and in public. At the agreed upon
moment during the parade, the women pulled out their "Torches of

Freedom" and smoked them in front of well-placed photographers. Bernays ensured that the photos made it around the world. From then on, cigarettes became symbols of "rebellious independence, glamour, seduction and sexual allure for both feminists and flappers."[4] Gloria Steinem would later use Bernays's tool kit to encourage rebellious independence, glamour, and seduction four decades later.

Steinem's Longevity

In her 1994 book *Moving Beyond Words*, Gloria tells her readers about the letter she has framed in her workspace at *Ms.* magazine:

> Above the desk where I write, there is a framed letter from Victoria Woodhull, the most controversial suffragist of them all. People who see her big scrawled signature assume I must be looking for inspiration in her life as the first woman to address Congress, the first to run for President, the first to originate and run her own weekly newspaper, and one of the few women to live out in public the principles of female emancipation and sexual freedom that were not only unusual in her day but illegal. All that is true...[5]

Gloria explains Woodhull's colorful life and dives into her audacity and her spiritualism, her free love proclamations, her Marxist leanings. And then she recounts how Woodhull finally just got tired, she and her sister Tennie moving to England, marrying titled gentlemen with lots of cash and sprawling estates. Steinem leaves out the part about how their finances were in a shambles and their reputations bankrupt. Victoria finally renounced her wild and wicked ways, including her free love platform. Gloria laments Victoria's turn, as well as the power that inherited money has to silence women.[6] But unlike Victoria Woodhull, Gloria

Steinem has never gotten tired of the role she chose to play as feminism's unanointed queen.

For decades Steinem has been promoting the spirit of Woodhull to every woman who will listen. What is striking about Gloria is her staying power. Other than the 2016 misstep by Lands' End, featuring Steinem in its catalogue geared mainly to traditional families—an ad that was later pulled from all channels after customer outcry[7]—Steinem has had incredible longevity in her career. As recently as June 2022, shortly after the fall of *Roe v. Wade*, she and Meghan Markle sat together with *Vogue* magazine, discussing their concerns as the debate over abortion policy returned to the democratic process. The two discussed their concerns and fears, as well as Gloria's own abortion. "I would have been stopped there," the eighty-eight-year-old confessed, ruminating over what would have happened if she had had a baby as a young single woman. "I was working as a waitress in London waiting for my visa to India, where I had a fellowship. I wouldn't have been able to do that. My life would've stopped there."[8]

Gloria's admission certainly isn't a new one, but what is new is that at eighty-eight, she is still talking, still drawing an audience, still "working." In many respects, Gloria is a symbol of what the feminist movement has been able to do: change, morph, and remain fresh.

Not all feminists appreciated Gloria's public relations genius. Betty Friedan resented her, seeing her as just a pretty face garnering the limelight, without intellectual heft.[9] Phyllis Chesler wrote of her candidly:

> What can I say about Gloria? Only this: My generation of feminists needed Susan B. Anthony but we got Mary Tyler Moore. We needed Harriet Tubman but we got Jane Fonda. We got the blonde, blow-dried feminist in the aviator glasses, the one in the skinny jeans, the feminist who posed in a bubble bath for People magazine. As glamorous as a movie

star, Gloria repeatedly gave the same pseudo-apology: "I'm not that attractive. I'm only attractive...for a feminist."[10]

Gloria and her perennial charm have kept feminism in the conversation. Her latest appearance with the Duchess of Sussex is evidence that she knows how to stay in the limelight. Chesler concedes that "Gloria has also kept feminism (and herself) fashionable by positioning and repositioning an ever-modified brand of feminism, one that is always in sync with the next media-favored movement."[11] Gloria is still morphing.

But there has been a lot more to solidifying feminism's privileged place in the culture than Gloria's famous leather pants. Second-wave feminism came onto the scene with the arrival of television. Feminists realized that they could use this medium for their own messaging. They also realized, using the tactics of the 1930s and 1940s Marxists, that they could infiltrate every American institution. And infiltrate they did. Today, there is scarcely an institution left that hasn't absorbed the feminist narrative in its entirety: Hollywood, politics, the fashion industry, book publishing, daytime television, magazines, academia, public schools, and now even Disney. Not only did they take over these organizations, but they found a way to silence their opponents, airbrushing most contrary ideas from any sort of cultural prominence.

Humiliation

Feminists have been able to squash the opposition, largely through humiliation or silencing. Phyllis Schlafly is perhaps the best-known woman who opposed the Equal Rights Amendment in the 1970s, with the likes of Steinem, Friedan, Bella Abzug, and the other well-known feminists on the other side. Not only was Schlafly maligned then, but a whole series—*Mrs. America*—was created around her, presenting her (via Cate Blanchett) as a cold-hearted upper class maven, obsessed with winning at any cost. Schlafly was presented in such an unappealing and one-dimensional light that even I found her off-putting in the final episode. While Blanchett pulled off Schlafly's likeness, the series made no effort to portray Schlafly as morally neutral or likeable. Blanchett has made no secret of her commitment to the sexual revolution. When she was asked, "What is your moral compass?" she responded, "In my vagina." (This was for a 2017 story that *Vanity Fair* subtitled "An International Women's Day Story for Everyone").[12]

Schlafly wasn't the first to be villainized. Feminists staged pranks, then known as "zaps," at a bridal show, where mice were released on the floor to disrupt the event, and protests at the Miss America pageant where underwear was burned to protest the objectification of women. Schlafly would later have a pie thrown in her face by an operative hiding as waitstaff at an afternoon luncheon.[13]

While pie-in-the-face is no longer trending, the internet has enabled Big Tech to attempt its own kind of "zapping," with YouTube channels mysteriously disappearing, Twitter accounts suspended without explanation, Facebook ads removed. The cancel culture is alive and well.

Fear

Feminists have also effectively unleashed the power of fear: "Without abortion women's future will be over." "Women will be saddled with children they don't want." "My body, my choice." And on and on and on, while they brandish wire hangers as symbols of what they believe were used in pre-*Roe* illegal abortions. Women are much more risk averse than men are, so tapping into the fear of bodily harm or vulnerability is highly effective. Psychologist Joyce Benenson says that the reason women avoid risks is simple: "An individual woman's survival and general good health are much more important than a man's. A man's basic contribution to procreation requires a few minutes of activity. Not so for a woman. A woman's body is responsible for successfully carrying the fetus to term, ensuring that it stays healthy. She then has to successfully give birth to her child, which is quite risky in humans. After birth, she has to feed her baby."[14] And on and on. "Fear is," Benenson adds, "a girl's suit of armor."[15] For many women, who have an inbuilt concern about health because of this element of human nature, abortion sounds a lot less scary, despite its many risky side effects that get little attention.

Steinem's most recent fear tactic, which goes well beyond the individual and the bodily, is to equate the end of reproductive choice with authoritarianism. "It should be taken for granted because if we don't have control of our own physical selves, we don't have a democracy," Gloria told NPR in 2021. "The problem is not the people who support abortion or who have had abortions. It's the people who oppose it and, therefore, are trying to take the first step in an authoritarian system."[16] This authoritarian system has taken on a mythical life in Margaret Atwood's *Handmaid's Tale*, proposing what we are supposed to believe such a tyranny will look like: the parade of women in red robes and bonnets who are presumably good merely because of their fertility, while their individuality and personalities are erased by forced conformity.

Fabricated statistics about how many women died before abortion was legal are also a perennial favorite. A feminist activist in Mexico just confessed that "we inflated the figures" of the number of women who were dying from botched abortions in order to decriminalize it. "At that time, I remember, we women said '100,000 women die from clandestine abortions.' It turns out that 100,000 people died in the whole country, men and women from all diseases. We inflated the figures."[17] Oops. This tactic, highly inflated mortality numbers, was used in large part to convince the 1973 Supreme Court to vote in favor of *Roe v. Wade*. Today, it remains a continually successful and predictable tactic.[18]

Feminism has also tapped into the natural human desire for freedom and independence. Steinem has repeated countless times throughout her career that she can't believe that women are still not in control of whom they have a child with and when. She reiterated her position again neatly, with palpable irritation: "I want women and men and everybody to be able to do anything they f——ing well please."[19]

But another part of feminism's success has been the trappings. Celebrities, politicians, journalists make it clear that without abortion we can only be headed to *The Handmaid's Tale*. Unless we smash the patriarchy, we are meant to believe that men will continue to suppress women all over again with their "toxic masculinity." The tidy fear-mongering narrative, the perfectly coiffed hair, the manicured hands, the on-trend fashions speak a convincing language of authority and truth, of a club or tribe of which only right-thinking women are a part.

Real science, meanwhile, gets a regular airbrush from the debate, especially on the topic of when human life begins, when a baby's heart starts beating, and when a baby can feel pain. Nary a consideration is given to the negative effects abortion has on women, such as the link between abortion and risk of breast cancer.[20] When making predictions about when climate change will destroy the planet, high-profile celebrities claim to pay close attention to science, but they don't seem willing to look at any abortion-related data that came after the 1970s unless they believe it helps their case.

The Tribe

Success of feminism can be seen in women's general fear of appearing to be out of step with other women. We generally see following the trends as a positive thing in the fashion industry, but trends are much bigger than what is coming down the runway or featured in *Vogue*. We see what celebrities are wearing, and we want to wear it. We hear what celebrities are promoting, and we want to promote it. Women, much more so than men, have the desire to conform to community pressure. The power of women's desire to fit in with other women and have their approval is probably one of the most unrecognized or undiscussed cultural pressures. Benenson says that fear of being left out of a group is one of the scariest realities for women: "Barring imminent death of herself or her child, nothing strikes more fear into the heart of a girl or woman than the thought that she will be excluded."[21] We can see this power in the life of Abby Johnson, who was the Planned Parenthood employee of the year in 2008 but who had a dramatic change of heart after witnessing a live abortion. As the film *Unplanned* chronicles, Abby's parents and her husband were decidedly against her work at the clinic. She was able to tune out those voices because of the affirmation she got from her work and the women at Planned Parenthood.[22] It is this kind of pressure that most women feel, to conform with other women, that decidedly shapes their thinking on women's issues. It feels good to agree with other women, which is some of the appeal of women's marches. There is something appealing about liking female celebrities, and we want to be women we think they would like. There is also something vital about being in solidarity with other women. The act of disagreeing with women, especially those whom one loves or esteems, feels rotten and can come with significant social consequences, particularly if brought out publicly. It is considered a betrayal, a slight, and it isn't something that is tossed aside easily as "just a difference of opinion" the way it often is for men who disagree with each other. These are the social strings that keep us tethered to the feminist agenda or tossed out into the cold, and they are remarkably powerful in instilling conformity on the ground level—at the gym, grocery store, office, playground, or coffee shop. We want to be part of the group. As a result, most women never consider that there might be a different way to live, to think about their lives, bodies, families, and careers.

In her book *Revolution from Within: A Book of Self-Esteem*, Steinem recounts her experience as a journalist being asked to leave the lobby of the Plaza Hotel in New York City in the 1960s because she was an unaccompanied woman. A few weeks later, several women picketed the Plaza Hotel for not allowing them to be seated for lunch without a man present at their table. There were injustices that needed tending to in the 1960s. But what she describes next is interesting. Once again, she had to meet someone in the Plaza Hotel lobby for a story, but this time, because of the witness of the other women who picketed the hotel, she had more courage. She calls this "self-esteem," but what she is describing isn't really about her self-esteem: it is about her finding her "tribe" or being encouraged by finding like-minded women, viewing their success, and seeing that she too could have the same success if she had the same courage. She says she was "catching the contagious spirit of those women who had picketed," and "by seeing through their eyes, I had begun to see through my own."[23] This is very different than self-esteem. It is finding one's tribe, club, a place of belonging. And it is a recognition of what people in that group do. Maybe this wasn't at the forefront of self-help books in the early 1990s, but Gloria was certainly onto to something: our tribes are vital to our flourishing, and they used to be made up of family, extended family, and community. Feminism is a jealous lover and has worked hard to make sure it is the only tribe to which every woman wants to belong.

CHAPTER 7

The Queen Bees and Power

Ruth Bader Ginsburg's death in 2020 filled our social media feeds with images of the iconic Supreme Court justice. Scrolling through her photos was a reminder that no one has worn black robes with such style and savvy. The second woman to be a Supreme Court justice, she exuded a sense of quiet confidence, deep intelligence, and an unmistakable panache.

Her pithy quotes included many wise notions:

- So often in life, things that you regard as an impediment turn out to be great, good fortune.[1]
- Don't be distracted by emotions like anger, envy, resentment. These just zap energy and waste time.[2]
- Women belong in all places where decisions are being made. It shouldn't be that women are the exception.[3]

- I just read Anne-Marie Slaughter's book. She talked about "we don't have it all." Who does? I've had it all in the course of my life, but at different times.[4]

She was the picture of refinement and style, with a biopic that left most of the audience thinking, "Every young woman needs to see this film." Surely she was a woman that every woman could get behind and emulate.

But what if there was a crack in RBG's thought? What if, despite all the trappings, she missed something fundamental? What if she wasn't always able to think independently but was caught up in the vortex of radical feminist ideas that dominate our culture? One popular RBG meme invoked her mother's sage advice, "My mother told me to be a lady. And for her, that meant be your own person, be independent."[5] By RBG's own standards—that is, to be your own person and to be independent—it is astounding how lockstep she was with the feminist movement. Her beliefs about abortion, for instance, were identical to those of the majority of women in mainstream media, Hollywood, the fashion industry, and politics. Perhaps at one time, early in her career, what she was doing was truly independent; but for most of her career, she touted the same ideas that we have been told would be "good for women."

Consider the strongest female influencers today, the top of the feminist heap. Most are now in their sixties, seventies, and eighties: Hillary Clinton, Nancy Pelosi, Elizabeth Warren, Whoopi Goldberg, Joy Behar, Anna Wintour, Oprah Winfrey, Ellen De Generes, Dianne Feinstein, Madonna, Maxine Waters, Jane Fonda, Christiane Amanpour, Sonia Sotomayor, Elena Kagan, and Terry Gross. These are America's "Golden Girls" or "Queen Bees." Despite many of these women being well past an age of retirement, they, like Gloria Steinem, still have a foot in the door and pull cultural levers, dictating who is cool and who isn't. For example, if Supreme Court justice Amy Coney Barrett had worn a lace collar on her black robes, the look that Justice Ruth Bader Ginsburg popularized would not have become quite so iconic.

Queen bees aren't a new phenomenon. One researcher calls them the "adult versions of the mean girls from school" who make the uncool miserable.[6] These women and their adherents are supposed to be the cool women. With the help of fellow cool women in the media, their warts and social gaffes are largely glossed over, such as Maxine Waters's telling homeless constituents to go home,[7] Elizabeth Warren's affirmative action achievements based on her Native American heritage,[8] or Nancy Pelosi's famous 2010 claim about the Affordable Care Act that Congress would have "to pass the bill so you can find out what's in it."[9]

Meanwhile, those who question, who think outside of the determined narrative, and who take issue with the queen bees' ideas are generally accused in the court of public opinion of sending women back to enslavement. There is no middle ground. Perhaps this is why we don't seem to apply the generational "don't trust anyone over forty" mantra of distrust to these women. Millennial women seem to be perfectly okay with having octogenarian women dictate how they live. It is fascinating to think of all the railing against authority that we have seen in this culture, but nary a peep has been voiced against the dominant authority of feminists.

The queen bees, because of their monopoly, have also become incredibly powerful. That power is protected, and it continually expands their reach and influence.

In addition to the press, they have a unique set of tools: smiles and euphemisms. Queen bees know how vital rhetoric and visuals are for the continued life of the movement. It's a movement built not on truth and reality but on smoke and smiles that hide the raw grasping at power, control, and greed, which often masquerades as care for women. "Women," Benenson explains, "can gather around smiling and laughing, exchanging polite, intimate, and even warm conversation, while simultaneously destroying one another's careers. The contrast is jarring."[10] The smile is a way of protecting against outright aggression, which might be dangerous for a woman. Euphemisms are effective in hiding the truth: "product of conception," "fetus," "pro-choice," "anti-choice." The language also gives the tribe a kind of insider's speak, uniting them more closely on a psychological level.

Queen Bee TV

In 1997, Barbara Walters launched *The View*, a television talk show for women. *The View* is supposed to be "regular" women sitting around talking about current events and issues related to life as a woman. Its success can be measured by the fact that it is still on televison today. Walters, who passed away in 2022, left the show in 2014, but two other original hosts remain: Joy Behar and Whoopi Goldberg. The show usually has five women on their regular chatty panel. But, of course, *The View* doesn't quite represent American women. It represents liberal American women. There are usually one or maybe two conservative women on the show—some closer to the center, such as Meghan McCain—but the show in all its years of airing has never given conversative women the majority. Conservatives, despite representing half of U.S. women, always remain the minority. If there were an actual balance, the liberal women wouldn't be able to control the conversation, and they might lose control of the studio audience, even when the "applause" sign is on. It is critical for them to push the belief that liberal women are the right-thinking set, while conservative and pro-life women are merely to be tolerated or teamed up against. As long as a gang of progressive women are in the majority, it is easy to keep this illusion alive.

The impression that everyone agrees with them is one the elites have relied upon for fifty years. Planned Parenthood president Alexis McGill Johnson recently used this tactic in an interview with *Forbes* by calling those who are pro-life "a small but vocal opposition," instead of recognizing that pro-lifers represent about half the country.[11]

Efforts to control the message go well beyond *The View*. In the 1980s, feminist magazine editors collaborated on talking points for articles in their various publications to sway women's minds, particularly on touchy subjects such as abortion, as Myrna Blyth has explained in her book *Spin Sisters*.[12] Famous "listserv" emails allowed elite journalists to craft and disseminate the narrative they wanted the public to consume. While the original listserv email might be gone, it isn't hard to see that something similar still exists because of the significant overlap in language among mainstream media outlets, and, perhaps more strikingly, the significant overlap on what they don't report. Perhaps the most curious example is the difference between the way first ladies have been covered at *Vogue*. Melania Trump, who was a model, never graced its cover, but Jill Biden was featured as soon they could get it to print. Supreme Court justice Ketanji Brown Jackson got the Annie Leibovitz treatment, with photos taken of her around the U.S. capital, while Justice Amy Coney Barrett did not.[13] Those who promote the narrative get star treatment, while those who thwart it, don't.

What Mean Girls Do

When Kelly Lester was a teenager, she had an abortion. Her boyfriend's mother drove her to the clinic. Thereafter, her life would never be the same. A nationally ranked tennis player, she dropped out of tennis. Her life spiraled into drugs, terrible men, and one bad decision after another. At some point, she got a job as a receptionist at the same

Planned Parenthood where she had aborted her first child. Part of her job was to make the pregnant women who came through the door leave "unpregnant." She tore out ads in the waiting-room magazines that might trigger warm feelings about being a mother, minivan ads, or ads for engagement rings. She was instructed to turn the heat up or down in the waiting room, making it uncomfortable for those who came with the pregnant woman to reenforce the pregnant woman's sense of being alone. *If this guy can't stick around for a cold waiting room, how could he ever help with a baby?* was the idea. And worst of all, she watched as women who had botched abortions returned to the operating table to be sterilized. Kelly, like so many others, thought she was working for Planned Parenthood to empower women. But what she found was not at all empowering. She found debauchery, denigration, and illegal violations of even the most basic human dignity.[14]

Another former Planned Parenthood employee, Takisha, describes witnessing infanticide after a child survived an attempted abortion:

> It was on my first day in the POC (Products of Conception) room that everything changed for me. I was responsible for assembling the dismembered babies, as well as cleaning the dryers, hoses, the speculum, and other instruments—all of it awful, bloody business—and putting me on edge immediately. But that was also the day they brought in a full baby on a tray, the one whose lips seemed sealed in permanent silence. I gasped when I saw him—a whole and perfect baby, like a doll. As I looked at him lying there, he suddenly moved. He was the first of many babies who came to me whole and moving their little arms and legs until they were taken away and put in a freezer. That was the extent of these babies' tragic lives. They were poisoned, plopped in a cold tray,

taken away in a bag, and frozen to death without ever being allowed a proper birth.[15]

The mean girls live and work in institutions well beyond Planned Parenthood. The sex-trafficking industry, aided significantly by abortion facilities that eliminate the natural consequences of sexual activity, and that don't ask pesky questions, is at an all-time high, with annual profits nearing $150 billion.[16] The industry is fueled by porn and the uninhibited sexual desires unleashed by the sexual revolution. Vulnerable immigrants are easy targets, particularly women and children—both boys and girls—who have their passports stolen when they arrive in the United States. They are drugged, sold repeatedly each day, filmed for porn, provided abortions when necessary, and put back to work as soon as the bleeding stops.

The fallout is also very real for poor and pregnant women. Kathleen Wilson has run Mary's Shelter in Fredericksburg, Virginia, for the past seventeen years, hosting more than four hundred women in crisis pregnancies. The shelter provides pregnant women and any other children they may have with a place to go for up to three years to get the support, love, and training they need to care for their families. Many of these women have been trafficked and prostituted; they have been drug addicts, victims of domestic violence, and/or experienced mental or physical abuse. Their wounds are deep and often affect every aspect of their life.

Wilson describes these women as being trapped in "bureaugamy," a relationship with the state rather than a husband: "In many cases, the state has been their mommy and daddy, so it's natural that it is now in the place of a husband, providing for their needs, so much so that they don't feel the need for a husband."[17] The brokenness of their situations is perpetuated by the fracturing of family, and the generational effects of fatherlessness in the home.

As for their relationships with men, "They aren't based on ever wanting to be committed to each other but are just based on desires."[18] Wilson adds:

> The state promotes and encourages a life with multiple part-ners without commitment, while also pushing abortion lib-erally. Women have the impression they are free to do what they want, but ultimately, they can't get what they really want—stability, security, and love. These are the things the state can't get them. While they are staying with us, they see and learn from real role models. And in the seventeen years, never once have I had one woman mention or show signs…that she regretted having a baby. Not one. Not one said, "I wish I didn't feel pressured into having this child." But I have had many who have cried about their abortions.[19]

All of these victims, the poor women, the trafficked, and the babies used for experiments or left to die after an abortion, are the poor among us. They are invisible, without a voice, but they are hit hardest by the decisions made by the most privileged women and men among us, those who have the resources to protect them from these awful realities. As Thomas Sowell said, "It is so easy to be wrong—and to persist in being wrong—when the costs of being wrong are paid by others."[20]

Most American women with money, degrees, or connections will never hear that our culturally prescribed feminist lifestyle is the source of their unhappiness, struggles, and feeling of emptiness. It seems that we just allow women to free-fall into truly awful states, without even so much as the quickly spoken warnings of side effects required for pharmaceutical commercials. (Imagine what that might sound like: *Side effects may include sexually transmitted diseases, debilitating depres-sion, loneliness, despair, substance abuse, and suicide.*)

What's Hidden

Feminist ideas, in their popularity, can feel unimpeachable. But some are beginning to challenge them, working around the usual established media avenues that won't touch them. One of these women is Kristan Hawkins, the president of Students for Life of America.

While on a campus speaking tour, Kristan debated a young pro-choice woman about abortion. The unnamed coed started by reading her own poster: "Life begins when you understand living women matter more than potential babies."

Hawkins asked: If it's a potential baby, what is inside of a woman?

Coed: It's a fetus.

Hawkins: Is it living?

Coed: No.

Hawkins: How can it grow if it's not living?

Coed: Actually, actually, that's like saying...an acorn is a tree.

Hawkins: When does the fetus become living?

Coed: (pausing) That's actually a good question....

Hawkins: Yeah, of course, because you don't know it, because it is living. It's living. You're fundamentally denying science to validate your opinion.

Coed: You, you, you actively, you actively deny science, ma'am.

Hawkins: How am I deny...What science did I deny?

Deflecting, the young woman points out other posters in the group of women supporting her.

Hawkins keeps pressing: "What science did I deny?"

And so the conversation goes for another few more minutes, but in the midst of it, the young coed looks to her friends, like a game show contestant desperately wanting their input. She looks disoriented, as if thinking, *How can this be going so badly? I'm using all of our best lines.*[21]

The exchange is interesting because of the force with which the young pro-abortion activist speaks followed by her incredulity at the fact that she isn't scoring points with her verbal arrows. They fall flat, or boomerang, coming back to make her look silly. It went so badly for her because pro-choice ideas are rarely debated in the public square. This is what happens when the tribe and the queen bees make sure no one looks behind the curtain. Scientific data concerning when life begins, or when a child's life is worth saving, elude our public narrative. Pro-lifers are willing to debate, but those on the pro-choice side know they will be trounced. They don't have reason on their side, just tired and old rhetoric.

Hiding the Truth

There are other ways feminists have protected the movement from close scrutiny. Most women have little interest in studying feminists, whether from earlier decades or the current day. They simply take it on good faith that feminism is right.

Feminists also tend to write in obscure and academic ways, which makes reading their work like slogging through mud. Most women don't want to out themselves and say, "I don't understand a word of this." Judith Butler is a prime example of writing in a way that is almost entirely impenetrable. Kate Millett's *Sexual Politics* reads like academic porn, though it was considered ground-breaking, brave, and brilliant, which is why she was featured on the cover of *TIME* magazine.[22]

A more prosaic type of hiding is the everyday fear instilled in the hearts of the cool girls that they will damage the movement if they complain about other women's terrible behavior. In *The Atlantic*, Olga Khazan wrote about bullying in the workplace. She was amazed at what she unearthed when she heard the vitriol of one woman on the receiving end of vicious and unreasonable female bosses:

> Her screed against the female partners surprised me, since people don't usually rail against historically marginalized groups on the record. When I reached out to other women to ask whether they'd had similar experiences, some were appalled by the question, as though I were Phyllis Schlafly calling from beyond the grave. But then they would say things like "Well, there was this one time…" and tales of female sabotage would spill forth. As I went about my dozens of interviews, I began to feel like a priest to whom women were confessing their sins against feminism.[23]

Feminist women also circle the wagons around each other, keeping what they think could damage the movement from the public eye, such as Kate Millett's mental illness. This is nothing new. For example, Mary Shelley's daughter-in-law burned a large number of pages of her journal, while Susan B. Anthony's biographer burned pages and pages of her work in a fire that was said to last for days.[24] Author Charlotte Gordon, in her book *Romantic Outlaws*, makes little mention of Percy Shelley's radical affairs that involved numerous women together. In the book, after Shelley's death, there is mention of Mary Shelley having a lesbian affair—a detail which seemed to come out of nowhere given the few details the book had previously offered.[25] It was only because I had read other books about Percy Shelley's various exploits that Mary's lesbian affair became intelligible.

Humor, much like pop music, is also frequently used to keep us in line. Political jokes, or jokes about men, sex, and reproduction, send a subtle message that if you aren't on their side, you'll become the butt of the joke. *Saturday Night Live* is a purveyor of this kind of humor, as are female standup comedians, most of whose jokes are too crass to include here. One critic gushes over comedian Jenny Slate:

> I first fell for Jenny Slate when she accidentally dropped the F-bomb on *Saturday Night Live*, and her career has only gotten richer and more interesting since she left the show. She starred in the 2014 abortion rom-com (yes, they exist!) *Obvious Child*, working much of her own stand-up into her role as the struggling comedian Donna; and her work with Gabe Liedman in the comedy duo *Gabe & Jenny* is consistently spit-out-your-wine funny. Plus, who can forget her role as Mona-Lisa Saperstein on *Parks and Recreation*?[26]

Comedy and pop music with a feminist slant have become the new avenues to convey radical ideals. In the same way that Percy Shelley used his verse to transgress taboos, comedy and lyrics are the new points of entry when tearing down convention.

The New Pirates

For centuries people lived with high stakes, ugliness, and the raw. The commonplace reality was perhaps best captured in the seventeenth century by Thomas Hobbes: Life is "nasty, brutish, and short." This is what life was like in the darker and lawless corners of the world, where pirates and thieves plundered with impunity.

The project of the twentieth, and now the twenty-first, century has been to chart a different course, to escape the crude and coarse, the rancid and sour, and to forestall the instant turns of fortunes. The unspoken but very real goal has been to make life "tidy, elegant, and long."

It seems like a noble goal. The problem is that the pirates are still with us. They're still stalking the children, still selling them (or their body parts) into a new kind of slavery. The pirate, a true scourge of the sea, wore his moral decrepitude on his body with years of hard living and fighting—a missing ear, a broken nose, scars from sword fights. He is frightening to look at. But today, instead of the warning of a grisly man in an eye patch with a cauliflower ear, we hear the melodic voice of the educated, discussing how much to charge for freshly aborted baby parts in between sips of chardonnay.[27] We see the manicured hands of the doctor vacuuming out the contents of the womb. We witness the well-branded Planned Parenthood clinics promising happiness while delivering pain and death. Instead of the clash of swords, we hear the familiar beep, beep, beep of the medical waste disposal truck backing up to an abortion clinic to retrieve what remains of children deemed unwanted. Well-heeled journalists, lobbyists, and union bosses fawn close behind, hoping for scraps from the table.

We have been lulled into thinking that all the millions of dead children are not a problem. In fact, they might just be the solution, the LEGO® box of spare parts for our medical needs or the wide array of other uses. We may have been successful in making life "tidy, elegant, and long," but the pirates are truly still with us, still plundering, lying, and slaughtering. Although they may be polished, creased, ironed, slicked, and starched, they know how to capitalize off the very young, the weak, and the defenseless. Thousands are killed daily in the form of abortion, with populations the size of Ukraine or Spain being wiped out each year.[28]

One might think the case is overstated, but the numbers tell a different story when compared with the deadliest "isms" of the twentieth century. The number of dead because of feminism quickly dwarfed Hitler's camps—roughly sixteen to twenty million—or Stalin's gulags (some have speculated twenty million).[29] Its most genius stroke was to kill, not through a standing army or messy camps, but one soul at a time, sometimes two, extinguished by their own parents.

CHAPTER 8

Patriarchy Smashing

For decades modern women have bought into the fashionable belief that our last frontier is the masculine world. This carrot of competing with and besting men has been dangled in front of nearly every Western woman since the 1960s. Today, the mantra has changed slightly: *Not only are we as good as men, we are in fact better at being men than they are.* So many commercials and ads directed at women confirm this. *Poor men, they wouldn't be able to do anything without us—clean up a mess, make a meal, purchase a new car.*

Since the time of Mary Wollstonecraft, the focus of feminism has been to tear down the male hierarchy. As we have seen, Wollstonecraft made no secret of her disdain for it, and feminists have followed her up to today. But this disdain for men has had a powerful engine behind it: victimhood.

We saw that Gloria Steinem and others zeroed in on women's emotions and heartstrings, often short-circuiting reason or logic. She knew how to communicate to women, how to motivate us to get moving on the social justice front. The essential piece used by feminists is the iron wedge between the sexes, tearing apart the united force of husband and wife and making them mortal enemies. Why? Because feminism's main goal is to convince women that our happiness resides in our being just like our husbands, that they have the better lot. And the engine used to catalyze these emotions, to drive her into action, is to show her how she has been victimized by men, just like so many women before her.

Women have been fed the idea that we are victims simply because we are women, and men are oppressors simply because they are men. Even if we aren't unhappy, we should be. We just aren't smart enough or haven't had our consciousness raised sufficiently enough to figure out why. Feminism came along to rescue us from our own ignorance with consciousness-raising groups.

Consciousness-raising is another idea from Marx that has been recommended for women who just don't realize they are miserable and oppressed yet. In 1897, the socialist paper *Lucifer* explained that its work was to "preach the gospel of discontent to women, to mothers and prospective mothers of the human races." "Women," the editor added, "are not awake to the fact that they are slaves—not conscious of their own degradation as individual human beings."[1] Consciousness-raising has been used in various forms ever since. During the second wave of feminism, the popular format was this:

> Consciousness-raising (CR) groups were composed of seven to ten women who might not have known each other beforehand or who might have met briefly on the barricades. These were not therapy groups. No one paid to be a member. We were not there to solve personal problems. The group's purpose was to help women recognize that we were oppressed so that we would engage in political activism of one kind or another.[2]

The groups explored all kinds of areas where women might have had some experience of being oppressed, including:

> Gendered training in childhood; the kinds of mothers and fathers we had; whether education was important for girls in our family; our adult sexual experiences;... whether we had ever been raped, had an abortion, married, or lived with a man; whether we had children and, if so, whether anyone helped us with child care, housework, and shopping; whether we had ever been attracted to another woman; and whether we were employed and, if so, had careers or merely jobs.[3]

It was quite the list with which to find grievances, but the end goal wasn't healing, clarity, or peace. The effort was intended precisely to stir a woman up, to enrage her, to make her see victimhood in even the most negligible places and motivate her to act. It is a kind of unrest, and a never-ending quest to find new ways to feed this victimization that ultimately is supposed to lead women to right all wrongs, according to the theory.

Certainly, there are women who have been victims of abuse. But these women need help and support, perhaps professional help, but not consciousness-raising that adds salt to their wounds. Quite often, however, the goal is to stir up previously unperceived problems, to create suffering, malcontent, and anger where none existed. Consciousness-raising, in effect, creates a kind of contagion. That is part of the efficacy of a group format. Even if a woman doesn't have grievances herself, she will hear about grievances from other women. In her compassion, she will be enraged for other women, which is a natural response, but again with the goal that she be provoked into rage for its own sake. Consciousness-raising isn't aimed at seeking justice, it is more activism to achieve perfect equality.

Envy and resentment are at the heart of these efforts, which seek to root them deeply in a woman's soul, targeting the unattainable male life to which she believes she is entitled. It rests on the belief that men and women can be exactly the same. This is also the same kind of striving for the unattainable that animates communism: the belief that if we just tinker with economics enough and get the proletariat angry enough, then everyone will somehow magically all be the same. "They [the proletariat] have been powered by a deep hatred of inequality and have aspired to create a more egalitarian social order," wrote Marx. The problem for both feminism and communism is that "the very passions that have been mobilized against oppressive inequality shade easily into envy, envy of a particularly destructive sort."⁴ Envy becomes the driver, especially when the grievances are slight and remote. The rage against the patriarchy has easily slipped into envy. Essentially, feminism argues, "We want what you have. You have power. We want your power. You have free love, or later, sex, without consequences. We want that too. You get to go out into the world for work. We want that also." It was a kind of tug of wanting to be everything that they believe men are and have—sex without consequences, adventurous careers, freedom from the burdens of home—while also wanting men to either become like women or vanish altogether. There are plenty of examples in the culture today, with pressure on men to call themselves feminists or the vitriol hurled at manly men, packed neatly into the phrase "toxic masculinity."

As any Marxist can tell you, it is easy to stir up discontent. It all sounds so rational and so fixable. *If only we were just all exactly the same.* But because it is driven by an ideology, the goal posts change and new problems emerge.

The real issue is that feminism has been trying to solve female problems with male answers. Psychologist Joyce Benenson explains:

The answer lies in women's focus. They must solve different problems than men. Women bear children. They must find some way to keep themselves and their children alive. They must ensure that their children live to reproduce. They must carefully select others who will provide critically important assistance. Even if a woman never has a child, she still sees the world through a different lens than a man.[5]

It is no small wonder feminism isn't a fix. The problems feminism started out wanting to fix have led to new problems, problems that are a direct result of their "fixes." Trying to fix the problems of women by erasing gender has now opened up a whole new can of worms.

The two ideologies can be seen in the use of economic disparities between men and women as a wedge, pointing out the injustice of the system and its supposedly inherent sexism. Communist Eleanor Flexner's book *Century of Struggle*, outlining the women's suffrage movement, brings this home with extensive discussion of women's wages in the 1800s, but this discussion is there to highlight the disparity of men and women in terms Marxists care about—economic terms.[6] The issue of "equal work for equal pay" is like a perennial soft spot to show how sexist the system is. This conversation is as heated today as it ever was, despite the fact that wage disparity, when comparing apples to apples, no longer exists. A woman who works her whole life as a professional and never has any children generally makes more money than a man does. But it has also been shown that the more children a woman has, the less she works outside the home, and the more children a man has, the more he works.[7] There are also significant differences in the kinds of work women tend to choose versus what men select. Body strength permits men to do a greater variety of jobs than women, and these jobs are often much more dangerous than those typically done by women. Women, meanwhile, often select educational paths and career trajectories that are more relational, and therefore less profitable than say finance or STEM-type careers (which are populated predominantly by men).

Phyllis Chesler also notes the fluid connection between feminism and Marxism. Chesler exposed the drama behind the women's movement—the betrayals, lying, cheating, and stealing that happened among these women trying to capture the national imagination. "If only we had known that suffragists had also fought hard and dirty and that politicians and ideologues behave this way, we might not have taken it all so personally," Chesler explained. "If only we had understood more about the dark side of female psychology, we might have been able to find ways to resist our own mean-girl treachery. If only. Only now, a half century later, do I understand that women in groups tend to demand uniformity, conformity, shoulder-to-shoulder nonhierarchical sisterhood—one in which no one is more rewarded than anyone else. Marxism and female psychology are a natural fit psychologically."[8]

The destructive envy women have toward men can be boiled down to simple terms: *We hate you, but we want to become everything you are.* It is a kind of envy, but also a hidden rejection of what it means to be a woman and a desire to become what they perceive men to be: powerful, without the demands or drudgery of mothering children.

This transvaluation of both men and women has created an odd dynamic between the sexes. Men aren't sure what to do, so they just try to "shadow box" the women in their lives while ignoring the most toxic women around them. Women, meanwhile, live in this schizophrenic relationship where they want to be what men are but also hate men. There is little indication that women are better at being men yet, but there is, as we will see, growing confirmation that the culture believes men are better at being women.

The end result is, of course, the belief in a zero-sum game, where if men are flourishing, women are not, and *vice versa*. Feminists refuse to move away from this binary way of thinking and recognize the delicate interdependence that exists among men and women. Instead, they continue, along with Gloria Steinem, to find fault or create fault in everything. "If you look at decision making in the household, which is more democratic than it used to be but not still completely democratic," Steinem says, "if you look at naming, though many women keep their own names, some women keep two names. Men don't. You know, I mean, it may seem minor, but it's pervasive."[9] Despite Gloria's concerns, it is simply impossible for everyone to flourish if we are trying to demean, belittle, destroy, or ignore half the population.

Submissive Men

Men, meanwhile, have also been silenced. One reality that has become clear is that men do not like arguing with women. This goes all the way back to Adam in the garden. But even the word "patriarchy" seems to act like kryptonite against men. A vague word—much like "racism" today—that has silenced much of the population. Few slogans have had as much staying power.

Women have also used victimhood and bullying to silence men. Men simply do not know how to respond to aggressive women's behavior. As Jordan Peterson explained, men know how to deal with each other in aggressive situations, but men don't know how to deal with women. Moreover, there is also the problem that women who have experienced terrible male behavior, those who have been abused and abandoned, who are broken and wounded—the lost girls—are often not even capable of discerning healthy male behavior. Peterson explains:

> Women whose relationship with men has been seriously pathologized cannot distinguish between male authority and competence and male tyrannical power. Like they fail to differentiate because all they see is the oppressive male.... Their experiences with men might have been rough enough so that that differentiation never occurred. Because it has to occur. And you have to have a lot of experience with men, and good men too, before that will occur.[10]

What happens when the movement in general has been characterized by lost girls, by women who are so broken that they can't discern toxic from healthy masculinity? Peterson believes that much of the tension between the sexes stems from this reality: "It seems to me that we're also increasingly dominated by a view of masculinity that's mostly characteristic of women who have terrible personality disorders and who are unable to have healthy relationships with men."[11] Young women who are highly influenced by the queen bees, by the lost girls, are getting the strong message that all masculinity is bad, unless they exercise it, because of this malformed view of men held by broken women.

Feminism also sold women on the belief they "can have it all," that whatever they want can be acquired and that life should be fun, pleasurable, lucrative, and exciting. But the piece of life that has been left out is what is real and inevitable: suffering. Sociologist Philip Rieff says there is an "instinctual renunciation" that most of humanity has understood about suffering.[12] Much suffering occurs because we are renouncing something that we want for a greater cause: the soldier in the midst of battle, the mother laboring to birth a baby, the parents sacrificing for their children's education and future, these are the "instinctual" kinds of sacrifices that people make for other people, for the greater good. But feminism has wiped away this "instinctual renunciation" and told women that they shouldn't have to renounce anything. This is how Whoopi Goldberg can say with a straight face that a baby in the womb is "a toxic thing" to a mother,[13] or Gloria Steinem can say the desire women have to serve others is "codependency,"[14] or Elizabeth Warren can accuse pregnancy resource centers of "torturing" women.[15]

The net effect of women's sense of entitlement, envy, and rage has been to turn us into a type of man that women hate, the negligent, narcissistic, aloof, unengaged man, like players and cads.

The New Fairy Tale

Fairy tales have been told across cultures and continents for millennia. More than simply an entertaining story, fairy tales are a culture's vehicle to share its values and underscore its most prized virtues. We know many of their familiar themes and patterns, having heard them since early childhood.

One recurring fairy tale plot is the evil queen or matriarch, as seen in "Cinderella," "The Little Mermaid," and "Snow White." This woman is envious of a younger and prettier upstart and will go to any lengths necessary to get rid of the threat. As the story unfolds, we know implicitly who the good characters are, as well as the villains. We know that the evil queen is not a victim, and her grasping at power and status makes her the purveyor of misery as she tries to destroy the life of the protagonist.

And as every little girl has done for millennia, we cheer when the queen's vile plans are foiled, and the kind and beautiful princess is finally free to live her life. The miserable matriarch's envy led to her own demise. This recurrent theme has its own moral: envy is called a deadly sin for a reason, for it will destroy the envious from the inside out.

As we have chronicled, feminism has rewritten this fairy tale's script. No longer is envy the downfall of women, but a badge of honor. And the ones we envy aren't younger upstarts, but men, and not the best of men, but men like Hugh Hefner or Don Draper. The fairy tale has told us that men have liberties that far surpass our own and are the real pinnacle of a life well lived.

This new fairy tale has its roots in the 1790s, with Mary Wollstonecraft's call to restructure society, to make men more like women and women more like men. For 150 years, women agitated against the patriarchy but never quite figured out a way to erase it completely. Then it happened, as if the magic spell had been discovered. Women found the secret way to bring down the patriarchy once and for all in Kate Millett's litany: destroying the family.

For over fifty years, women have been clamoring to make themselves into men—mentally and now biologically—but in the scramble we have frittered away what it means to be a woman. The solid ground that used to be beneath our feet has eroded into the sea, leaving nothing to stand on. Our identity has been cobbled together with this grasping at manhood, while what it means to be a woman has dissolved and is now an unanswerable question. There's no place left to see what womanhood is, so enshrined have we made the male model and the neutral notion of person, human being, or individual. In our envy, women have been erased.

The fruits of envy haven't just targeted men but also children, the needy, demanding upstarts whom we are told are the real obstacle to our happiness. Following the mantra of manhood, the seed has been deeply planted that no woman should have to mother another. Mothering sets us back. Mothering enslaves us. This is the pro-choice fairy tale, complete with a parade of the victimized women in red robes and white bonnets, reminding us just how awful and enslaving motherhood is.

But what the red-robed and well-heeled women don't understand is that, try as they may to rewrite the fairy tale, those agitating for something other than womanhood will never be the protagonists. Envy cannot make a hero, only an oppressor. The model we have followed has locked us into a caricature of ourselves, resembling the evil queen who not only destroys herself but everyone else around her with her grasping at power and control. It's precisely her abandonment of all the things that could make her happy that are her—and our—downfall, classic elements such as kindness, service, love, compassion, tenderness, and graciousness.

The power of the new feminist fairy tale is highly compelling, but it comes at a cost. The millions of women who have followed it blindly find themselves trapped in a world they didn't expect, barren and broken, with hearts aching for more. This often manifests as rage and fear. Margaret Thatcher observed: "The spirit of envy can destroy. It can never build."[16] Feminists have failed to offer a future to build in their quest to purge the warts of the past. Yes, surrogates can be found—pet parents with fur babies—but the structure of mothering is built deeply into our bodies and souls, despite our scarce acknowledgment of it.

The stories we tell are powerful. The saddest part of all is that we have been taught to envy our very children, who are made for our love not our spite. Until we women can abandon our envy-driven identity, we will continue to rage, resent, destroy, and demean those for whom we were made to love and care.

What we are living through boils down to something shockingly simple. Where feminism has taken the place of religion, the queen bees are the stand-in for the clergy, preaching the gospel of discontent, narcissism, self, worship, and human sacrifice. It has become the "cool" religion where the elites and celebrities worship (and are worshipped).

We started this book looking at Mary Wollstonecraft and her lamentations about the vices of women. Her main concerns were that women of her day were coquettish, too focused on vain pleasures like clothing and beauty, too intent on having a small appetite, too engrossed in alluring men, while remaining mis- or undereducated. Well over two hundred years later, women appear to have many of these same vices, despite the overwhelming effort to reshape and reform the minds of women.

Men cannot claim to be improved either, despite the frequent reproofs and rebuffs that come with smashing the patriarchy. There still seem to be plenty of cads and boors to go around, mistreating women and neglecting their children, despite the overwhelming effort to reshape and reform the minds of men. Tossed aside, largely because they are not required to win the heart or body of a woman, are the concepts of commitment, self-mastery, self-sacrifice, and family, and many of the practical virtues that accompany them: generosity, patience, wonder, awe, gratitude, perseverance, reverence. In some ways it has been a race to the bottom: a question of who can behave worse, with women behaving just as boorishly as (and sometimes worse than) the men they have criticized in previous generations.

As Louise Perry explains, "A monogamous marriage system is successful in part because it pushes men away from cad mode, particularly when pre-marital sex is also prohibited. Under these circumstances, if a man wants to have sex in a way that's socially acceptable, he has to make himself marriageable, which means holding down a good job and setting up a household suitable for the raising of children. He has to tame himself, in other words."[17] The benefits don't end there. "Fatherhood…has a further taming effect," says Perry, "even at the biochemical level: when men are involved in the care of their young children, their testosterone levels drop, alongside their aggression and sex drive. A society composed of tamed men is a better society to live in, for men, for women and for children."[18] Now "tame" might not be the right word to use. Men aren't wild animals. "Virtuous" might be better because it respects a man's dignity and implies that he has the interior capacity to direct his life and behavior instead of having it foisted upon him from the outside. It is through a man's exercising of virtues that he can best protect, defend, provide for, and love those who have been entrusted to his care.

PART III

No Girls

What happens after fifty years of indoctrination into the idea that men and the male lifestyle are intrinsically superior to the lackluster life of ladies? Most feminists didn't expect that biological men would boomerang back into the female world. But gender-bending and malleable human nature don't have to move in just one direction. The feminist request that men become more like women has finally materialized, although not in the way they expected.

This is where we truly begin to see the effects of centuries of hollowing out what it means to be a woman, yet we can see its origins in the oft-repeated line that females are human beings, but nothing more specific. What started innocently enough with Mary Wollstonecraft—and the claim that women are human beings and not chattel or slaves—took on a different meaning. As the meaning of womanhood was emptied of particulars, the overarching terms "human being" or "people" were adopted to define "woman" without resorting to any female characteristics. This allowed females to be spoken of in a way that referred to their dignity but not to their sex or characteristics associated with their femaleness. Feminism used this understanding frequently to emphasize its own goals:

> **Mary Livermore:** "Above the titles of wife and mother, which, although dear, are transitory and accidental, there is the title human being, which precedes and out-ranks every other."[1]
>
> **Elizabeth Hawes:** "Females, as well as males, are human beings."[2]
>
> **Betty Friedan:** "Perhaps it is only a sick or immature society that chooses to make women 'housewives,' not people."[3]
>
> **Marie Shear:** "*feminism*: the radical notion that women are people."[4]
>
> **Radicalesbians:** "A lesbian, according to the feminist group, is any woman who seeks to be a 'freer human being than her society' commands..."[5]

"People" and "human beings" became a shorthand for referencing women without reference to motherhood, homemaking, being a wife, or anything else that might point to what most women have done throughout history, even if the content of those activities has changed in dramatic ways over time. Women have become the embodiment of Percy Shelley's Cythna. This usage has led, in large part, to the inability of most of the Western world to define what a woman is.

The sad reality is that playing these games on an elite level has had terrible results for everyday people, particularly for young girls who might not fit in or are socially awkward but intellectually bright, who are ground zero for the transgender craze and surgeries. These are the girls whom the gender pageantry is raining on the hardest. These are the girls who will continue to pay the steepest price for what they believe to be an ideal: getting rid of their female bodies.

CHAPTER 9

Margaret and Ls

The twentieth century was marked by literary and artistic women with lives touched by, even if not entirely given over to, lesbianism. Names such as Gertrude Stein, Frida Kahlo, Virginia Woolf, and Simone de Beauvoir come to mind. Hidden in the shadows and still illegal, lesbianism—or the "love that dare not say its name"—was a part of the American underbelly.[1] It was forbidden, which for some, like Kate Millett, made it all the more appealing, another taboo to take down.

The civil rights movement exploded back into the culture in the 1960s. Like the abolition movement before it, feminism inserted itself into the conversation, equating women's rights with those of blacks. This time, however, there was another movement that attached itself to these two: the gay rights movement. Same-sex attraction is older than the hills, but what was new about the movement was its effort to inject the sexuality of same-sex couples into the cultural conversation about equal rights.

Early activists came up with slogans describing homosexuals as "an oppressed cultural minority"[2] and asserting "Gay Is Good"[3] to create the perception in the minds of the general population that sexuality that was other than hetero was just another oppressed minority, that it too was good. However, as Camille Paglia has noted, the history of pre-Stonewall gay identity reveals a population explicitly choosing to reject bourgeois norms of sexual morality, and framing an identity around transgression and rebellion as a conscious thing.[4] But the movement got started to decriminalize gay sex and to end the raids on gay nightclubs, bathhouses, and lesbian bars. Over time, it morphed slowly: normalizing same-sex relationships then became an effort to give same-sex relationships the same status as heterosexual couples, including not just civil unions, but the unprecedented effort to call same-sex unions "marriage."

The gay rights movement also seemed to have a fresh voice with science at its back. Armed with the data from the Kinsey Reports and the work of Doctor John Money, who invented the term "gender identity," gay activism was on the precipice of something that had never happened before—becoming mainstream. Much of the work of both Money and Kinsey has been discredited because of their suspect methodology and illegal practices, including sexually abusing infants and children, but few knew that at the time.[5] Kinsey, for example, instructed men to have pedophilic relationships with children as young as two months old. Their cries of protest and pain were reported as achieving orgasm instead of as the afflicting torture.[6]

A first major turning point for gay liberation came on June 28, 1969, when patrons of the popular Stonewall Inn in New York's Greenwich Village fought back against ongoing police raids of their neighborhood gay bar. After a police raid, as patrons were being rounded up to be taken to jail, a lesbian, handcuffed because she had struggled against her arrest, yelled out, "Why don't you guys do something?"[7] Chaos ensued, as one witness described:

It was as though her question broke the spell that had, for generations, held gays and lesbians in thrall. "The crowd became explosive." ... "Police brutality!" "Pigs!" they shrieked. They pelted the police with a rain of pennies (dirty coppers). Someone threw a loosened cobblestone. Beer cans and glass bottles followed. Bricks from a nearby construction site were hurled at the squad cars with baseball-player skill.[8]

The outnumbered police ran for their lives back into the Stonewall Inn, with several officers lucky to escape when it was set ablaze. The riot lasted for days, with a carnival-like atmosphere setting in as people came in droves to protest for their rights, with the police keeping to the peripheries. Dancing transvestites capture the mood:

They were met by a Rockettes-style chorus line of queens who linked arms, kicked high, and to the tune of "Ta-ra-ra Boom-de-ay" bellowed sassily, "We are the Stonewall girls / We wear our hair in curls / We don't wear underwear / We show our pubic hair / We pick up lots of tricks / That's how we get our kicks / We wear our dungarees / Above our nelly knees."[9]

Suddenly, the movement experienced a great shift psychologically and became more aggressive, although the movement, like feminism, was split between those trying to make homosexuals seem like everyday Americans and those letting the more colorful side of the movement, such as the singing transvestites at the Stonewall riots, become the prevailing voice of their efforts. But also like the feminist movement, the gay rights movement created a sense of tribal loyalty; both the lost girls and the lost boys finally had a home and a sense of solace in finding each other and having their voices heard.

Although gays and lesbians were frequently associated together because of their same-sex attraction, there was a deep divide between the two groups, each branching off in different directions. Lesbianism effectively became a branch of feminism, with one commentator suggesting that "lesbianism is where feminism goes if it stays on track,"[10] eventually tossing aside men altogether. Lesbian Martha Shelley wrote, "I have met many, many feminists who were not lesbian—but I have never met a lesbian who was not a feminist."[11]

Not surprisingly, feminism's radical nature in the '60s lent itself to the radical nature of the lesbian movement. "The new lesbians had no connection to the old-school lesbians...those who thought that if only lesbians would mind their manners, they'd be given a place at the table. The new lesbians didn't want a place at the table—they aimed to trash the whole dining room."[12] Many of the women in the feminist movement who started out as heterosexuals ended up coming out as bisexual or as lesbian. Kate Millett publicly admitted that she was a lesbian and for her there was no going back. "'Say it! Say you are a Lesbian.' Yes I said. Yes. Because I know what she means. The line goes, inflexible as a fascist edict, that bisexuality is a cop-out. Yes I said yes I am a Lesbian. It was the last strength I had."[13] Others such as Angela Davis, Phyllis Chesler, Andrea Dworkin, and Robin Morgan visited various stages of gender fluidity, difficult to track.[14]

While politically lesbian activists maintained a relationship with activists who were gay men, most considered it a relationship of convenience to bolster numbers and to fight a common enemy. Lesbians, however, saw themselves as very different from gay men, for men at large were the enemy. "Frustrated with the male leadership of most gay liberation groups," one history of the movement explained, "lesbians influenced by the feminist movement of the 1970s formed their own collectives, record labels, music festivals, newspapers, bookstores, and publishing houses, and called for lesbian rights in mainstream feminist groups like the National Organization for Women (NOW)."[15] This mainstreaming of the movement was a hard sell for many years, especially with Betty Friedan as a highly vocal and active opponent of including lesbians in NOW. But the lesbians were undeterred and showed up as "the Lavender Menace" at the Second Congress to Unite Women in 1970. A flash mob of lesbians attended the event, and when the lights were turned out briefly, they revealed their lavender T-shirts, while shouting their agenda. Despite the humiliation of that event for Friedan, it would take an audience of twenty thousand women at the 1977 National Women's Conference in Houston for Friedan to relent on the lesbian question.

The Power of Zaps

One organization, the Gay Activist Alliance, decide to take a page from the feminist playbook by using public humiliation to get the opposition to cave to their demands. They recalled how the feminists had used such tactics to protest the Miss America pageant—when women threw away their bras, makeup, hairspray, and girdles—or their release of rodents at a bridal show. "Zaps," as they were called, were premeditated pranks to make fools of those perceived to be the bad guys. They "were playful, mischievous, and dead serious, all at once."[16] Friedan was certainly the victim of one with the Lavender Menace flash mob, mentioned above.

Singer Anita Bryant threw her voice and endorsement against a gay rights proposition in Florida in the late '70s. When the proposition was voted down, activists in other states were waiting for Bryant and found ways to "zap" her publicly whenever they could, including throwing a banana-cream pie into her face on live TV.[17]

Whenever there were intense political tensions or an impasse, "zaps" were trotted out. In 2010, when the "Don't Ask, Don't Tell"

policy was up for debate, activists protested by handcuffing themselves to the White House fence to raise awareness of the supposed
unfairness of men serving their country but not being allowed to say
that they were "gay" in the U.S. military. The policy was reversed later
that year.

Another highly successful move used by the LGBT+ propaganda
arm is to project extremely controversial suggestions while simultaneously normalizing smaller, albeit still controversial suggestions. Much
like retailers dependent on deep sales, they set their retail price much
higher than the price they need, so that when they do have a sale, they
can get by. By moving the goalposts on an idea, the culture is then
distracted from small incremental achievements, otherwise known as
"shifting the Overton window."

Ellen DeGeneres came out as a lesbian in 1997, with Rosie
O'Donnell following in 2002. Both appear to have been later pushed
out of their popular TV talk show work when it came to light that their
off-screen personas weren't nearly as likeable as they were on-screen.
TV shows such as *Glee, Modern Family*, and *Will & Grace* contrib-
uted to America's "evolving stance on gay marriage," as evidenced by
President Barack Obama, who came to support legalized same-sex
marriage during his presidency.[18]

What is remarkable is just how quickly America went from a
country committed to a culture in which marriage between a man
and a woman served as the bedrock of a strong society to one that
dramatically embraced the LGBT+ ideology. The movement was
effective in framing its struggle as another category of human rights
issues, arguing that granting rights to the LGBT+ population was
reasonable, rational, and a common-sense approach to the emotions
and desires they experience. Slogans such as "Love is Love" and "You
can't help who you fall in love with" seemed to win the day. The real
nail in the coffin, however, was *Obergefell v. Hodges*. The Supreme

Court decision forced the debate in one direction after only five years of serious contention—and not because of a unified, national change of heart. How this decision came about, not surprisingly, is also connected to feminist activism.

Margaret Sanger

Margaret Higgins was born in September 1879 in Corning, New York, the daughter of a socialist sculptor and a busy mother who was raising eleven children. She grew up to become a nurse and married William Sanger. They had three children, and their early years sounded very happy. "It was all very pleasant, and at first I was busy and contented. The endless details of housekeeping did not seem to me drudgery; conquering minor crises was exciting. Though I was never slavishly domestic, I was inclined to be slavishly maternal," Sanger wrote in her autobiography.[19] But something changed when the family moved back to New York and then to Paris. Their home became a hub for socialists, liberals, and anarchists, including Walter Duranty. Sanger became deeply interested in the question of "birth control," a phrase she helped coin.[20] The concept of birth control, however, was not new. The journal *Lucifer* from the late 1800s, founded by Moses Harmon, had been advocating for birth control and free love for decades by the time Sanger was promoting the notion; its name was eventually changed to *The American Journal of Eugenics*. Sanger believed, like Harmon, that if poor, needy, hungry, and unhealthy children could be prevented, then the world could inch closer to a utopian paradise. She put forward her panacea without mincing words:

> The creators of over-population are the women, who, while
> wringing their hands over each fresh horror, submit anew to
> their task of producing the multitudes who will bring about

the *next* tragedy of civilization. While unknowingly laying the foundations of tyrannies and providing the human tinder for racial conflagrations, woman was also unknowingly creating slums, filling asylums with insane, and institutions with other defectives. She was replenishing the ranks of the prostitutes, furnishing grist for the criminal courts and inmates for prisons. Had she planned deliberately to achieve this tragic total of human waste and misery, she could hardly have done it more effectively.[21]

While they were living in Paris, the Sangers' marriage fell apart, and she moved with the children back to the United States, until her work came under the gaze of law enforcement because birth control was still illegal. She fled to Europe, leaving her children in the United States to be cared for by others. There she came into contact with other birth control proponents and Malthusians, who promoted the idea that the world would soon be wildly overpopulated, another theory that since has been widely debunked. But Margaret felt deeply that the answer to women's problems—and, more broadly, all of civilization's problems—was the use of birth control. For Sanger, birth control, eugenic control, and population control were the three spokes of a better future.[22] In her book on Sanger, Angela Franks explains, "Sanger believed that certain classes of people should not be parents, and if they would not embrace a childless state voluntarily, it should be forced upon them."[23] Someone had to stop these women who "went on breeding with staggering rapidity those numberless, undesired children who become the clogs and the destroyers of civilizations."[24]

In the early 1910s, Sanger proffered her ideas to feminists, who were then mainly focused on the suffrage push. They found her proposal less than appealing. Her rhetoric of calling a mother "a breeding machine and a drudge… [that's] a liability to her neighborhood, to her class, to society"[25] probably did little to win them over. She pitched it to a more friendly audience, the socialists and communists:

> When I suggested that the basis of Feminism might be the right to be a mother regardless of church or state, their inherited prejudices were instantly aroused. They were still subject to the age-old, masculine atmosphere compounded of protection and dominance.
>
> Disappointed in that quarter I turned to the Socialists and trade unionists, trusting they would appreciate the importance of family limitation in the kind of civilization towards which they were stumbling. Notices were sent to *The Masses, Mother Earth, The Call, The Arm and Hammer, The Liberator*, all names echoing the spirit which had quickened them.[26]

In 1914, Sanger started a newsletter, *Woman Rebel.* "My initial declaration of the right of the individual was the slogan 'No Gods, No Masters.' Gods, not God. I wanted that word to go beyond religion and also stop turning idols, heroes, leaders into gods. I defined a woman's duty, 'To look the world in the face with a go-to-hell look in the eyes; to have an idea; to speak and act in defiance of convention.'"[27] Her ideas caught on, but she continued to be plagued by law enforcement. Eventually, Sanger founded the American Birth Control League, which would later become Planned Parenthood Federation of America. Feminism finally started to take notice, and Planned Parenthood eventually became the flagship for the movement, making abortion readily available for women when their birth control failed— inevitable reality.

What does this have to do with sterile lesbians? Birth control is the key to understanding how homosexuality went from being unacceptable to being actively embraced by American culture. At first glance, this may seem preposterous. How could something that homosexuals don't need swing the general opinion about homosexuality? Sanger and birth control, particularly the arrival of the Pill, transformed sex in the American and Western mind. Prior to these generally effective, though certainly not foolproof, ways of controlling birth—something previous generations of feminists could have only dreamed of—sexuality was always tightly connected in people's minds with fertility. Sex meant children. With birth control's arrival, sex no longer had to include children. Sex could be only about pleasure and uniting a couple together, through the release of significant bonding hormones. Suddenly, sex could be about feelings and pleasure it produced without any concern for babies. It took a while for the childless notion of sex to take hold of culture, but as the LGBT+ movement made inroads, people began to ask themselves: *How is their sex any different than ours? We do it for pleasure. They do it for pleasure. We don't have children unless we want to children. They don't have children.* Fertility and babies became terribly passé unless one was actively trying to achieve pregnancy or if something didn't work as promised. It became so passé in fact that many countries, such as Japan, Spain, China, and Italy, now have below-replacement-level birthrates. The true problem isn't overpopulation but underpopulation, with many countries experiencing birthrates under the replacement levels, leading to several demographic crises. These are not surprising realities when women have been told that their children will hold them back, that their husbands are a menace, that their happiness lies in work rather than motherhood, and that they should leave the home and have lesbian relationships. Plummeting birthrates should surprise no one.

The Dirty Bomb

Earlier we saw the endgame of Wilhelm Reich's sexual revolution, but his effort to sexualize the whole family was loaded up like a dirty bomb. Beyond the initial blast, there were other damaging elements that would make it all but impossible for society to return to the traditional family and recover what had been the status quo for centuries. Reich developed a new idea of abuse, primarily concerned with the psychological level rather than the physical. Reich argued that it is abuse if one's sexuality is repressed or one's sexual desires are left unaffirmed. Reich agreed with Freud that our sexual well-being is based on our sexual satisfaction. If these needs are not met, Reich suggested, one is oppressed.[28] "Once oppression becomes primarily psychological," Carl Trueman explains, "it also becomes somewhat arbitrary and subjective."[29] This is the root of our culture's current fixation on victimhood, which has become arbitrary and subjective; it can be based on something as simple as someone feeling "unsafe" when a wrong pronoun is used, or someone being "triggered" by a pro-life speaker. Suddenly, entire institutions are supposed to jump into action to rectify the "abuse." Trueman explains the broader effect:

> This is why arguments about sex that default to statements such as "It is nobody's business what consenting adults do in the privacy of their own home" miss the point. Sex is no longer a private activity because sexuality is a constitutive element of public, social identity. Matters of private sexual behavior are not simply private; they are public and political because they constitute a significant part of how our culture thinks of identity. And it is only through public acknowledgment of their legitimacy that those identities are recognized and legitimated. To outlaw, for example, gay sex or merely

to tolerate it, is to outlaw or merely tolerate a certain identity. Both are ultimately forms of oppression, albeit the one more overtly so than the other.[30]

This remarkable transition of abuse from well-being, particularly that of the body, to the psychological and the mental has had dramatic effects. People are left without any way to guide their moral judgments other than with their emotions, and those emotions are protected at all costs because not to protect them would be abusive. This notion of abuse explains why the gay rights movement hasn't been content with acknowledgement but demands to be affirmed in the belief that homosexual behavior is equal to heterosexual relationships, in marriage and beyond, including the adoption of children and the use of surrogacy.

Flying

In her book *Flying*, about the rise of the lesbian movement, Kate Millett chronicles her own life from the moment she outed herself as a lesbian through her life as a lesbian and feminist activist. She remained married for many years to her Japanese husband, Fumio, despite her belief that bisexuality is a cop-out. Eventually, the jealousies and constant turntable of her lesbian relationships damaged her marriage. She identified this as the problem with free love at the beginning of the book:

Even with our most outrageous notions, free love for instance, we were hardly the first; Shelley and his friends had a try at that a hundred and fifty years ago. A student of mine at the experimental college, after spending a semester struggling with the idea of sexual union and property, concluded that until we could handle jealousy there wouldn't be much hope for progress. Probably there still isn't. Under the banner of antimonogamy there's a fine lot of sexual energy and experiment in *Flying*, but people still get hurt. Fumio [Millett's husband] didn't want to "transcend" monogamy; neither did Bookie [a lover]. The problems still remain, are with us every day, and we seem no closer to solving them.[31]

Millett seems to be something of a pinball, bouncing around from bed to bed, relationship to relationship, without any real meaning or purpose to any of them beyond fleeting pleasure and comfort for a deeply lonely and terribly broken woman. She is far from alone as a lesbian in lifestyle. In many respects these relationships without purpose were a foreshadowing of the hookup culture, the stream of ephemeral relationships built on extracting pleasure from others. Millett's life reminds us of feminism's parallel track, that, like Millett's, the movement was spurred on by youthful energy, curiosity, and folly. Kate's radical break with taboos, put high on the pedestal of the culture today, has collapsed down into conformism.

CHAPTER 10

Simone and T

Many years ago, Nordstrom featured a new marketing slogan: "Reinvent Yourself." It conveyed that it's time to change up who you are with a whole new look—which, of course, included a whole new wardrobe. But it wasn't just about getting women to buy new jeans, blouses, and beauty products; it spoke to something deeper in our culture: the desire for self-creation. To create a whole new me, to make for myself a new life. More recently, Meghan Markle talked about trying to affirm the self-creative capacity in little girls, so they could *"create a life greater than any fairy tale you've ever read."*[1] The desire to recreate the self in new and subversive ways is fundamental to the feminist project.

Becoming a Woman

Simone de Beauvoir and Jean-Paul Sartre developed existentialist philosophy, which placed a premium on being authentic to oneself and radical freedom no matter what that might entail. It was an anti-rational way of thinking, with results gauged by feeling, not reason. For Simone, self-creation was vital in order to be true to one's authentic self, otherwise one's life is merely conforming to outside demands.[2]

In de Beauvoir's essay "Must We Burn Sade?" she analyses the work of Marquis de Sade, who shows up once again. De Beauvoir claims him for the existentialist movement because of what Debra Bergoffen and Megan Burke characterize as his "authentic ethics and a politics of rebellion" that can usher in a utopia of freedom. She also applauds de Sade for "uncovering the despotic secrets of the patriarchal political machine."[3] The problem with de Sade, however, that de Beauvoir cannot quite get past is his violation of others' liberty. After all, he did advocate the maniacal and torturous treatment of others. While she praises his authenticity, de Beauvoir saw his cruel ethical violations as going beyond the limits of self-creation. As with Wollstonecraft, Mary Shelley, and other early feminists, free love lost its luster when the hard edge of biological reality emerged.

De Beauvoir continues her effort to explain female authenticity in her expansive work *The Second Sex*, arguing that women have not been permitted to be real women but some kind of incomplete male. Her most famous line is "One is not born, but rather becomes, woman."[4] She continues, "No biological, psychic, or economic destiny defines the figure that the human female takes on in society; it is civilization as a whole that elaborates this intermediary product between the male and the eunuch that is called feminine."[5] The culture has formed women, through convention and patriarchal power, to be stuck between the potency of men and the impotency of a castrated male. The way to free ourselves, in her view, is to break free of convention as well as biology. She advocates freeing ourselves from our human nature, focusing on our most authentic self. This separation of body and soul was the first step in opening the door to transgender theory. If the meaning and nature of the body can be erased, anything is possible, as long as it seems to be in accord with one's self-determined authentic self.

John Money's work on the sliding scale of gender theory was later added to de Beauvoir's work, allowing for the "discovery" of whole slew of genders, independent of the body. Although his work was discredited because of the sexual and psychological abuse he inflicted on his child patients in the name of his "research," the idea was already out of the barn and persists today, acknowledged as if it were sound psychology.

What we see today is de Beauvoir's claim taken to its logical extreme. If one "becomes" a woman, rather than womanhood being part of female human nature, then perhaps men, too, can "become" women. Women could likewise become men, once sex has been detached from the anatomical weight and confines of the body.

De Beauvoir's most famous statement has also led to the feminist theory that male and female are simply social constructs, further buttressing the idea that feelings or expression of gender are reality. Judith Butler argues that de Beauvoir's use of the verb "becoming" is the cornerstone of gender as a social construct. Butler explains that "if gender is something that one becomes—but can never be—then gender itself is a kind of becoming or activity, and that gender ought not to be conceived as a noun or a substantial thing or a static cultural marker, but rather as an incessant and repeated action of some sort."[6]

To make sure that the dots are not connected between a woman's biology and who she is as a woman, gender theorists have maligned the notion of "essentialism," arguing that a woman cannot know anything about who she is based on her body, her womb, breasts, or hips. These parts of female biology have become dispensable because they now seem useless. No one could have imagined how this would play out when de Beauvoir was writing in the mid-twentieth century, but twenty-first-century technology has made biological "gender transitioning" a reality.

Self-creation and self-expression are now entirely dependent on the mental identification of the individual, and, therefore, anything that encroaches on the internal feelings of another is considered abuse. This is why those who identify with the opposite sex are handled with such care, giving rise to new words like "birthing person," "parent A" and "parent B," "bleeding person," and "chest-feeder" so as not to offend anyone who defines themselves as a trans person, although there's scarcely any concern that the rest of us might be offended.

Becoming a Man

Imagine being built like Michael Phelps, with a long torso, arms and legs that slice through the water. Early in life, however, everyone around you starts insisting you should be a jockey. Swimming is no longer trendy, and anyone with any kind of sense knows that you should be racing horses. Encouraged by friends and parents alike, you and your body, which is totally unsuited for horse racing, head for the arena to jockey up. For years, you do everything you can to be the best jockey but are greeted only with failure, because no horse can fly like the wind with you on its back.

Those among us with a Michael Phelps physique instantly know we should never be encouraged to race horses. Now, unlike radically altering our bodies, the moral stakes of Michael Phelps jockeying a horse badly are relatively low. However, what is evident is that our bodies impose some limit on our identities. The physics and the mechanics tell us immediately that the Phelps physique and jockeying not mix. But what if that wasn't good enough? What if someone built like Michael Phelps was determined to become a jockey using new technology to remove some of his legs and attach his feet to his knees? Perfect. Well, maybe. But the question remains: Why the tortured, risky, expensive surgery to do that which one is not naturally wired to do?

Before thinking this is far-fetched, consider surgeries aimed at so-called gender transition, especially the removal of forearm skin for phalloplasty, which is the cobbling together of skin to create a faux penis. Most of us still have eyes to see distortions of human nature within the context of sports, but do we still have the capacity to see human nature—its physics, mechanics, and purposes—in male and female bodies? One well-documented current trend—a sort of social contagion among high school and college women—is to venture into the world of testosterone (T) injections and gender fluidity.

Prior to 2012, there was no research literature on adolescent girls presenting with gender dysphoria or rapid-onset gender dysphoria (ROGD). Abigail Shrier, in her book *Irreversible Damage*, explains this transgender craze among adolescent girls, and points out its correlation with the anorexia, bulimia, or cutting crazes of previous generations. Patterns have emerged among these girls, most of whom never showed any discontent with their bodies until adolescence. The typical sufferer is usually intelligent but somewhat socially awkward and doesn't quite fit in with the other girls. Curiously, she also doesn't really want to be a guy. These girls, Shrier explains, "make little effort to adopt the stereotypical habits of men; They rarely buy a weight set, watch football or ogle girls.... They want to be seen as 'queer,' definitely not 'cis men.' They flee womanhood like a house on fire, their minds fixed on escape, not on any particular destination."[7] As one therapist put it, "A common response that I get from female clients is something along these lines: 'I don't know exactly that I want to be a guy. I just know I don't want to be a girl.'"[8]

Shrier points to the arrival of smartphones as part of the engine for ROGD: "Teenage girlhood in America is practically synonymous with the worry that one's body does not measure up."[9] This sense of inadequacy has been exacerbated by the minute-by-minute reminders, brought to girls courtesy of a smartphone. "Social media personas—that is to say, the 'friends' most relevant to today's teens and with whom they spend the most time—admit no such imperfection," says Shrier. "Carefully curated...photographs set a beauty standard no real girl can meet."[10]

These girls are grasping at "T" (both testosterone and trans identity) as the panacea that will abate their suffering. The steady threat to parents, mentioned by both the heavily indoctrinated girl, and ideological psychologists and social workers, is that if she doesn't get the breast binder, the hormones, or the surgery, then she will kill herself, despite evidence that suicide rates go *up* after girls take these measures.[11] We are supposed to believe that going with "T" and a new name and identity will help girls avoid the suffering associated with indignities of womanhood, such as periods, weight gain, fertility, and unwanted sexual attention. This is the promise of "T." Being trans also has the added cache of being very in vogue at the moment, with praise and attention coming from just about everywhere, including President Joe Biden.

One of the most troubling issues is the unproven record of "puberty blockers" that are sold to work like a "pause" on a girl's development, but it isn't as tidy as just hitting a pause button where everything freezes in time. The long-term side effects are not fully understood because no long-term studies have been done. A girl on testosterone will also have her fertility threatened. Testosterone significantly dries out a uterus and risks vaginal atrophy. Other damaging effects include the shortening of vocal cords, significantly changing the girl's voice, the growth of hair on the chest and face, and male pattern baldness.[12] The unknowns of these supposed "treatments," and the hastiness with which they are applied to young girls, means that many will become locked forever into a new identity—promised, at least through certain stages, that the side effects are reversible.

Part of the horror of this craze is that psychologists and patients are calling the shots, not parents and medical doctors making a diagnosis, recommending treatment, and making informed decisions. The order of treatment has been inverted by the threat of suicide, but also because of the priority the culture has given to people's feelings about their gender. Any threat of feeling unsafe is enough to make people act imprudently. Beyond any kind of desire to serve women, the transgender craze is a cash cow. Vanderbilt's Clinic for Transgender Health recently ended its gender-surgery program after one of its employees was recorded at a conference explaining just how much money these surgeries, the follow-ups, and recurrent hospitalizations due to infections would rake in for the hospital.[13] Planned Parenthood has added another source of cash flow to their bottom line by administering body-altering hormones, the cherry on top of their history of exploitation and greed.[14]

One might object, *If this is what makes these women happy, why not?* There likely is a spark of excitement or relief that comes from heading, herd-like, to a Planned Parenthood clinic, receiving affirmations and encouragement from friends and employees, not to mention the ability to be regaled as a hero by the elite, including the president of the United States. Fashions and trends of dress and thought are like that. There's a type of satisfaction in joining the crowd and appearing to be "in," particularly for the young, impressionable, and socially awkward. But these are not the prelude to true happiness.

Girls are making decisions about themselves at a stage of life when peer pressure and the desire to fit in are steepest, but also at a time when it is hard to know who one is, even without the gender questions floating in the culture as an unwanted but unanswerable question. Moreover, the brain's frontal lobes don't develop fully until the mid-twenties or even thirties. This is the heart of the "executive functions" of the brain, such as planning, memory, and controlling impulses.[15] Vicki Thorn, founder of Project Rachel, a resource to help women grieve abortions, noticed that many of the women she helped developed tremendous guilt around age twenty-six after obtaining an abortion as a teenager.

Thorn realized that this is also the stage when the frontal lobes are finally fully mature; it was their newfound mental maturity that allowed these young women to finally have a sense of the gravity of what they had done.[16] There are plenty of reasons why we shouldn't let minors do whatever they want, particularly when it comes to something so weighty as sex and gender, and many of them hinge on the reality that their minds are not yet fully mature.

Porn's Handcuffs

The sexual revolution ushered in a broader effort to sexualize young women and children. Sexualizing teenagers started in the 1980s with the arrival of *Seventeen* magazine followed by *Teen Vogue*, which introduced highly sexualized content to minors. More recently, the reach of this sexualization extended even to preschool children, plying them with LGBT+ propaganda. Seemingly innocuous shows such as *Peppa Pig*, *Pete the Cat*, and *Blue's Clues* now feature alternative lifestyles and families, while drag queens remain committed to reading books to kindergarteners. Pornography, readily available on smartphones, has taken sexualization to a new level for both children and adults, and porn addiction has played a significant role in enslaving young people in the trans movement. In addition, the prevalence of trans influencers on social media makes the trans lifestyle attractive, and the pressure from the trans community ventures easily into cult-like behavior—especially with the vehement advice to cut off any family member, parents in particular, who disagree with a child's decision to embrace a trans lifestyle. There is a lot of power in affirmation from an online community, with trans influencers plying children with porn, sexual deviancy, and the occult. One mother wrote a heart-wrenching sketch of what had happened to her daughter when all of these tactics were used against her:

And the trans identity is not something that [a] child deter-
mines on her own. Rather, it is carefully manufactured and
cultivated on the internet and in peer groups, like a tended-to
plant.... Her personality changes to be sullen, combative and
disengaged. She is no longer jovial or interested in much of
anything unless it [is] related to being trans.

My daughter's crush, the girl who identified as a boy
and was 3 years older than my daughter, had sent her a
10-minute video of herself masturbating.... Yes, I had child
pornography on my device. That older girl...described in
intimate detail female anatomy and orgasms to a group of
some 6 or so 13-year-old girls online. This girl admitted to
having been sexually abused as a child. She admitted to being
obsessed with pedophile cases and serial killers. Now, she
was passing that abuse onto my child and other kids.

The young girl followers treated this older girl as a sage....
My daughter got interested in the dark arts, because that is
what this older girl liked. My daughter started asking for
everything that this older kid liked—a tarantula, a throne,
various records, a nose ring—you get the idea.

I now knew why my daughter had become unrecognizable. The history on every device was filled with pornography,...violent porn.

My daughter had been sucked into the dark web.

She was only 13.

After several tries, I stripped my daughter's phone of
all internet access. I stripped her school iPad of the most
egregious sites. I bought a safe and locked up all the phones
and devices. I got her a new phone number so that I could
block all of the pedophiles and groomers with whom she
was in contact.

The mother described how she "started calling random contacts from her phone. There were adult men answering.... Strangers from other states." But even with the removal of internet access, the nightmare continued:

> I would love to say that was the end of it. But, you see, the plant that grew from the groomers could not be cut down so easily.... She ran away, stating that I abused her because I blocked the internet....
>
> This week after finding yet another stowaway phone, my daughter offered to transform back to being a traditional girl—wear bras, grow her hair out, wear stereotypical female clothes, tell everyone to use her female name—in exchange for access to the internet with limited controls. Is she so addicted to porn that it trumps her alleged "trans identity"?[17]

One way to keep children stuck in this trap, as with this young girl, is to weave together the trans identity and sexual addiction, making it difficult to see them apart from each other. In this girl's case, the sexual addiction became the stronger of the two pressures, revealing how being "transgender" wasn't as stable of an identity as many would have us believe.

The sexual revolution has done a lot of damage to men, women, and children, but this new effort mutilates the female body in ways that cannot be reversed. For the women involved, it will take them to a place where, like it or not, there is no going back. There is no way to restore functioning breasts once they are removed. There is no way to restore proper function after a bottom surgery has been performed. There is no way to return a uterus back to the original once it has been dried out with years of testosterone use.

The long march to androgyny has allowed women to cut them-selves off from the very things that can lead to flourishing and happi-ness. True flourishing requires that something act in accord with its nature. But like the misled jockey with a Michael Phelps physique, women have been told that their happiness might reside in being a male and, as de Beauvoir and subsequent feminists argued, that the female body has no meaning. For over fifty years, we have been telling young girls it is better to be a boy. Now that we have the technology to approximate such a change, why should we expect them to want to be girls? Women continue to chase to the ends of the earth after any trend that promises happiness, yet we continue to reject the very things for which we are made.

Mary Shelley's Legacy

Each day technology gets closer to what Mary Shelley and her Doctor Frankenstein dreamed up, but, remarkably, this new technology, this spark of life and miracle of science, has had a similar effect. Doctor Frankenstein created his abominable creature out of a desire to undo the death of his mother, but the creature he ended up creating, all eight feet of him, was rejected by everyone who could see him, even his own creator. Doctor Frankenstein is aware throughout the novel that he has crossed a terrible line, and looks on in horror as the creature, real-izing that he could never be loved, slowly and methodically murders everyone associated with his unloving master. He finally hunts down Doctor Frankenstein and kills his creator. But that revenge was not enough. Despairing that his life's only purpose was now complete, he departs into the icy wastes of the Antarctic to incinerate himself on a pyre. Like Dido of Carthage, the monster dies, more alone than at the moment of his "birth."

We can look back to the creations of Mary Shelley, developed at the hands of Frankenstein, the cobbling together of body parts, hacking and sewing to make something new. It bears a frightening similarity to the images of young girls, fresh from double-mastectomy surgeries, performed on healthy tissue, motivated by the desire to be someone, anyone, different. Or at the arms missing a significant chunk of skin, removed for phallic-creation surgery. The Frankenstein-esque scars tell their story of how we, too, have become entranced by the desire to play God, to create and craft at will.[18] It wasn't enough for the creature; will it be enough for us?

The feminist movement has eviscerated our homes, our children, our lives as wives, our fertility, and now finally our bodies, leaving us in a strange no-man's-land—or rather a no-*woman's*-land—where we are simply a generic "human being," a traumatizing blank slate imposed over natural realities.

Many of the decisions girls and women make about their futures are decided when they are very young and not thinking about becoming mothers, or when they are in their twenties and thirties, at the height of their physical potential and when they are the least vulnerable if they don't have children. They are not thinking about what happens when they grow older and their health declines and their nuclear family starts to die out. When young women are congratulating themselves that they have not taken on the burden of childbearing, they are not thinking of their own future vulnerability. When they are least vulnerable, the inevitability of the future seems too far away to care about or consider, yet then they are shocked, horrified, and saddened by the reality into which they grow, but are now too old to rectify.

In roughly 350 BC, Aristotle wrote that women were deformed males. For centuries, men and women of goodwill have articulated the true nature of woman. But twenty-four hundred years later, willingly but unwittingly, we have proven Aristotle right, intentionally turning women into a pale reflection of the worst men in our society.

The LGBT+ Brand

For decades, Marxists have maligned the connection capitalism makes between the bourgeoisie and material goods, such as automobiles or suburban houses. In his book *One Dimensional Man*, Herbert Marcuse wrote, "The people recognize themselves in their commodities; they find their soul in their automobile, hi-fi set, split-level home, kitchen equipment."[19] Perhaps unwittingly, Marxist followers in the LGBT+ movement have done something similar. Instead of commodifying products that give people a sense of meaning and identity, they have commodified the body. Like the car manufactured with various options and features, now the body and one's identity can be tweaked according to various gender options and features. No longer limited to male and female, the latest LGBT+ flag has over forty different symbols from which one can pick and choose based on emotions and preferences. The exploitation Marxists were critical of in capitalism is now inflicted directly on the human body by those very Marxists. Beyond your grandmother's feminism, the contemporary movement is branded and marketed to pull in just about everyone, like it or not. The pride flag can be spotted everywhere, especially on car bumpers or woke coffee shops, from government agencies down to grade schools. In the month of June, Pride Month, corporations must fly the pride flag colors and promote pride in their marketing, including children's brands, or face the wrath of the cancel culture. Commodifying the body according to one's sexual tastes, which can be invented and re-invented at will, like a Frankenstein monster, has become the ultimate ideological brand, blending the powerful—and, some would argue, tyrannical—concepts of reinvention, emotion, marketing, and big money.

PART IV

The Way Home

There is a smugness about our culture today, in which elites have a sense not only of entitlement but also of superiority. Much of it comes from the daily affirmations they receive from like-minded thinkers, but it also relies on a general ignorance of history and its vicious lash. Few of us have lived through a hot war, famine, poverty, or significant natural disasters. We have lived during one of the most peaceful and prosperous stretch of decades in all of history. This relative calm offers false confidence, an ignorance of just how quickly things can go wrong. Certainly, the COVID-19 pandemic offered us a glimpse of our fragility, and many have reordered their priorities accordingly, but there are plenty who continue to live as if this kind of peace and prosperity is just the way life has always been in the past and always will be in the future. Our technology and full bellies have satiated us into thinking things will always be this way.

Sociologist Philip Rieff wrote a book in the 1960s anticipating this mindset. The book *The Triumph of the Therapeutic* predicted that in our culture "to be entertained would become the highest good, and boredom the most common evil."[1] Such a culture, Rieff continued, lives with the false confidence that there is "nothing at stake beyond a manipulatable sense of well-being."[2]

Many of us live in blissful ignorance, believing that the world can go as it will and we can act as we wish without any ramifications. Lost is a sense that the personal goes well beyond our local nexus of contacts, and the effects of our vices aren't limited to our friends and family. "We believe," says Rieff, "that we know something our predecessors did not: that we can live freely at last, enjoying all our senses—except the sense of the past—as unremembering, honest, and friendly barbarians all in a technological Eden."[3] The technological Eden of which Rieff speaks meets our every emotional whim, affirming us in isolated communities, or sexually satisfying us with images and virtual reality. How long can such a culture shoulder the weight of a civilization?

CHAPTER 11

Restoration

In her book *The Case against the Sexual Revolution*, Louise Perry writes about marriage:

> The critics of marriage are right to say that it has historically been used as a vehicle for the control of women by men, and they're right to point out that most marriages do not live up to a romantic ideal. They're right, too, that monogamous, lifelong marriage is in a sense "unnatural" in that it is not the human norm. The marriage system that prevailed in the West up until recently was not perfect, nor was it easy for most people to conform to, since it demanded high levels of tolerance and self-control. Where the critics go wrong is in arguing that there is any better system. There isn't.[1]

What Perry and other critics of marriage have missed is that marriage isn't just about children. Marriage is essential for building a healthy and growing civilization. Monogamous marriage is vital.

In the 1920s, J. D. Unwin, an English ethnologist and social anthropologist at Oxford University and Cambridge University, decided to look at monogamy and civilization. Unwin, an atheist, sifted through eighty primitive tribes and six known civilizations over five thousand years of history, including the Sumerians, Babylonians, Egyptians, Assyrians, Persians, Hindus, Chinese, and Romans. The results published in his 1934 book, *Sex and Culture*, surprised even the author. In his research, Unwin found that the greater a culture's sexual restraint, the greater that culture's accomplishments. Monogamous cultures could build and grow, produce art, music, architecture, and science, expand economies, and create space for people to flourish. But Unwin also found that as soon as a culture abandoned monogamy, particularly pre-marital chastity, it collapsed within three generations (he estimates each generation to be thirty-three years). "Any human society," Unwin wrote, "is free to choose either to display great energy or to enjoy sexual freedom; the evidence is that it cannot do both for more than one generation."[2] Unwin describes what he called "monotonous repetitions" of the decay followed by every one of the cultures he studied. "It is difficult to decide which aspect of the story is the more significant: the lamentable lack of original thought which in each case the reformers displayed, or the amazing alacrity with which, after a period of intense compulsory continence [sexual restraint], the human organism seizes the earliest opportunity to satisfy its innate desires in a direct or perverted manner."[3]

Human energy is at the heart of Unwin's research. There is only a limited amount of energy in a human person. When a culture abandons monogamy, Unwin explains, "sexual desires could then be satisfied in a direct or perverted manner.... So the energy of the society decreased, and then disappeared."[4] Sexual freedom continues to expand, as we have seen in our own culture, pushing into the earliest years of childhood. But that comes at a cost, says Unwin: "Conversation, literature, drama, art, science, cookery, furniture, architecture, engineering, gardening, agriculture—these and all other human activities are winnowed by its [sexual freedom's] gentle breeze."[5] Consider how much of the focus in our culture is spent on issues related to sexual freedom: abortion, birth control, health care, gender "transitioning," divorce, children from broken homes, deadbeat dads, overworked moms, and on and on. But if limits are put on sexual impulses, Unwin writes, "a limitation of sexual opportunity...produces thought, reflection, and energy."[6] These are the elements that build, while sexual liberation decays.

Unwin also saw that "in human records there is no instance of a society retaining its energy after a complete new generation has inherited a tradition which does not insist on pre-nuptial and post-nuptial continence."[7] Unwin saw repeatedly that as cultures became prosperous and adopted liberal sexual mores, they lost cohesion and a sense of purpose.

Each person has a limited amount of time, focus, energy, money, intelligence, and so on. How we spend them, according to Unwin, affects not only us, but travels at least to the third generation beyond our existence.

Perhaps the best example of sublimating energy is the monastic system, credited to Saint Benedict as the Roman civilization was crumbling. Celibate men, focusing their energy on work and prayer, not only preserved key elements of the Roman Empire but also established and built over many centuries expanding industries and new developing technologies, such as the scholastic system, the scientific method, agricultural advances, hospitals, and universities.

Unwin found that once pre-marital chastity was abandoned, within one hundred years society would also abandon monogamy, theism, and rational thinking. This is perhaps the most chilling of his insights, because it speaks to the state of our own culture. Belief in God, marriage, and even rational thinking have all gone by the wayside, giving way to the ever-changing feelings of the individual.

Unwin also saw that once a culture tipped in this direction, civilizational recovery was impossible, largely because of the elites' control over messaging. The state of any civilization, Unwin saw, "depends not on the behaviour of the majority (who often are almost completely controlled by their unconscious minds) but on that of a small minority who display their inherent powers."[8] A culture can only be as good as its elites; they directly influence how "the masses" behave. There is certainly plenty of evidence of this in our own culture, and the feminist narrative's success is clear evidence of it. We have "fallen in line" with their agenda.

Unwin's research coincides with the work of English historian Arnold Toynbee, who published his vast survey of twenty-seven dead civilizations, *A Study of History*, shortly after Unwin—in twelve volumes between 1934 and 1961—and argued, "Civilizations die from suicide, not murder."[9] Civilizations are hollowed out by their own decadence instead of being pulled down by outside aggressors.

Once these stages of decline set in, Unwin did not see a single civilization that was able to reverse its course. A small group of elites controlled the message, while the majority was silenced. The last two centuries have witnessed the prognostications of Marx, Marcuse, Reich, and Millett, who have promised enlightenment and utopias that men and women of goodwill have bought into; but none of what they espoused elevated civilization, rather it has worn civilization down into a tattered and threadbare mettle. While the message of Unwin and Toynbee feels like one of defeat, there are glimmers of hope that civilization will not collapse under the weight of Marx and his followers.

Worlds Apart

Perhaps the biggest obstacle facing those of us who want to see a restoration of our culture, a return to the family, to healthy and honored womanhood and motherhood, and widescale de-sexualization, is the wide gap separating us from those who want to maintain their crafted narrative. It goes much deeper than the merely political.

Whittaker Chambers's book *Witness* opens with perhaps one of the most heart-tugging forewords of all time, titled "Letter to My Children," in which he describes the wonder of his daughter's ear. The soul of Chambers was stirred in a way that often only the tininess and innocence of a child can offer. The awe and wonder of creation reached into his soul with the clear realization that even the smallest of ears was not created by man.

Beyond the tenderness addressed to his children, Chambers's foreword offers a key, or even *the* key, to what has led us to this point. In writing about communism, he describes what it is not:

> It is not simply a vicious plot hatched by wicked men in a sub-cellar. It is not just the writings of Marx and Lenin, dialectic materialism, the Politburo, the labor theory of value, the theory of the general strike, the Red Army, secret police, labor camps, underground conspiracy, the dictatorship of the proletariat, the technique of the coup d'état. It is not even those chanting, bannered millions that stream periodically, like disorganized armies, through the heart of the world's capitals: Moscow, New York, Tokyo, Paris, Rome. These are expressions of Communism, but they are not what Communism is about.[10]

Chambers goes on:

> Communists are that part of mankind which has recovered the power to live or die—to bear witness—for its faith. And

it is a simple, rational faith that inspires men to live or die for it.

It is not new. It is, in fact, man's second oldest faith. Its promise was whispered in the first days of the Creation under the Tree of the Knowledge of Good and Evil: "Ye Shall be as gods." It is the great alternative faith of mankind. Like all great faiths, its force derives from a simple vision. Other ages have had great visions. They have always been different versions of the same vision: the vision of God and man's relationship to God. The Communist vision is the vision of Man without God.

It is the vision of man's mind displacing God as the creative intelligence of the world. It is the vision of man's liberated mind, by the sole force of its rational intelligence, redirecting man's destiny and reorganizing man's life and the world.[11]

Chambers reveals why there is so much devotion to communism, why individuals have thrown themselves into it with reckless abandon, foregoing family, children, friendships, and pleasures of life in order to support the movement, almost like a secular saint embracing the ascetic. The difference, of course, is that the movement does not sacrifice back, it does not love back. Bella Dodd, who had been the chief communist organizer of public school teachers and unions, said of communists, "This was their cause, their life, their religion. They gave it everything they had all the time."[12] Unfortunately, the movement gave nothing back to them.

Chambers's summation illustrates that these two threads we have been tracking throughout several centuries are the same impulse, treading in that land of the "second oldest faith," where man is above God. There is only one way to explain the mayhem, vehemence, and violence that have been associated with the feminist ideology: for many, it is a religion and one that worships man instead of God.

Rieff has a helpful explanation for the cultural struggle in which we find ourselves. He breaks up history into three parts. The "first world" is the era of the ancient Greeks, when the world was determined by fate and the capricious will of the gods. The "second world" is that of faith in the one God. And the "third world" is the modern era, in which man is the locus of worship.[13] Rieff's analysis and terms—unrelated to the economic terms with the same names—help to explain why it is such a challenge for those of us who believe in God to engage in meaningful discourse with those who do not believe in God. There is no longer a common language for us to speak to each other, so instead we speak past each other. We saw this most especially in the debate over gay marriage. The second world people, whom Rieff calls "religious man," know that there is a human nature–based rationale for marriage as immutably defined between one man and one woman. The third world adherents, or "psychological man," view gay marriage as a question of civil rights and argue that they should be allowed, like heterosexuals, to love whomever they want. There is very little common ground for the two groups to communicate in the same language. Rieff explains why: "Religious man was born to be saved; psychological man is born to be pleased. The difference was established long ago, when 'I believe,' the cry of the ascetic, lost precedence to 'one feels,' the caveat of the therapeutic. And if the therapeutic is to win out, then surely the psychotherapist will be his secular spiritual guide."[14] It should then come as no surprise to us that psychologist Jordan Peterson has the kind of cultural clout that he does. He speaks the language of the therapeutic, thankfully in a way that leads people away from it, instead of deeper into its enslaving dungeons.

One point that Rieff makes clear, however, is that third world cultures are inherently unstable. They are not built on a sacred order or moral laws but on ever-shifting psychological states, trends, and emotions. "No culture in history," Rieff writes, "has sustained itself merely as a culture, however attractive and authoritative." A culture needs a sacred order to maintain it, which is what the commandment of monogamy is. Third world cultures "assault all sacred orders and their *agent/cultures*."[15] The second world and the doctrine of creation "is turned by the third [world] elites into a doctrine of de-creation in which the new world is a series of more or less horrible or at least horribly clever pastiches and negations of the complete and ever completing" sacred order.[16] As such, because the third world has no God left, "that world is nothing except its art. The delivery of those arts, its lifestyle, is everything. There is no world apart from that lifestyle."[17]

The second world, on the other hand, despite how it is depicted by the third, is never static. Rieff explains, "Sacred order is not static. The worlds created in their sacred orders are never complete. They are always being re-created by readers of what is hidden in those worlds so to create worlds within worlds; the hidden meaning of the world as it has never quite emerged before."[18] What Rieff means here is that when God acts in history, he is not repeating himself but continually doing something new, eliciting wonder, awe, fear, reverence. The Old and New Testaments attest to this, as do the varied lives of the saints.

How then do we rebuild and restore what was lost? Certainly not with more of what has already been tried and failed. What will restore what is lost is doing the opposite of what was done to tear us down. Restore monogamy. Restore the family. Restore the patriarchy. Restore the home. Restore motherhood. Restore children to their parents. And restore faith in one God.

Rieff says that "the death of a culture begins when its normative institutions fail to communicate ideals in ways that remain inwardly compelling."[19] This perhaps, more than anything discussed so far, is the solution to a collapsing culture—to do the hard work and to explain within our institutions why these ideals are compelling, finding new and fresh language to show that these institutions don't exist for their own sake but for ours, and for the future of our civilization.

CHAPTER 12

Mother

Gloria Steinem often repeated a story about an outing with her college geography class to a river. Gloria spotted a rather large turtle that was working its way up a hill toward a road. Concerned that the turtle would get run over if she made it to the road, Gloria picked it up, walked it down the hill, and put it back in the water. Her professor quietly said to her, "You know that turtle has probably spent a month crawling up the dirt path to lay its eggs in the mud on the side of the road—you have just put it back in the river."[1] Of course, Gloria felt terrible. While she had the best of intentions, she did absolutely the worst thing for this turtle.

Gloria's story was to remind her audience that we must do what is authentically good for people, not what we might think is good for them. This is a lesson we all must learn. It is a reminder that we have to pay attention to human nature and not just the human nature we want people to have, even if our view of human nature is much different than Steinem's.

Most every woman who ascribes to feminism does so because she truly wants to help women. She wants women to have better, happier lives. This is a good thing. The problem is that feminism didn't ask the right questions, so we got the wrong answer. And like Gloria's turtle, we've been put back in a place where we are worse off than before.

The question then becomes, what really helps women? To let women be women. But this is an incredible challenge when the whole context within which we have thought of ourselves is competition with men. We don't have easy answers to this question of what makes a woman a woman.

Years ago, my small daughter asked me what is better about being a girl than a boy, and I didn't have an answer. That little question got me thinking and working through the actual attributes, gifts, virtues, and qualities of women that we sweep under the carpet because they aren't in fashion. What we need as a culture is a new grammar, a new way of speaking about women altogether beyond the sterile "she's a human being" rhetoric. We need to look at ourselves as body and soul, working together, and to consider women within a context and a family instead of as an island amid a sea of people.

As uncomfortable as it is to say, we have to consider women as mothers—even if, of course, many among us aren't mothers now or won't become mothers. All women are called to a type of psychological or spiritual motherhood in our relationship with others, where we look out for the best interest of others, mentor them, and help them grow. We have to come to know ourselves, who we are, not as victims, but as real women: learning where our strengths are, how to understand vulnerability instead of pretending it doesn't exist, where to direct our desire to control, how to set boundaries and order our ambitions.

We need to restore the importance of serving others, not to control them or be controlled by them, and not in codependency. Certainly, women serve others for these reasons. But we have to get back to what service really means. German philosopher Max Scheler spoke of serving others this way: "This great urge to love, to serve, to bend down, is God's own essence."[2] There is something divine about wanting to give of ourselves, of wanting to improve others' lives, to help them reach their potential, and affirm their goodness. A dear friend of mine used to say that children—and, in the end, all of us—need to know that there is "someone dialed in to us," someone who is paying attention, who notices when our demeanor changes, who can tell when we are struggling with something without our saying so, who can see what we need, sometimes even before we know we need it.

It is readily apparent when digging into the history of feminism that there is a remarkable absence of discussion about children, about what it means to be a mother, about what a relationship with a child is like—the highs and lows, the tender moments, the small victories, the quickly passing years, the awe of watching a tiny child grow into adulthood, the friendship born of love, challenges, and shared history that comes, especially after passing through adolescence. None of these things are mentioned in feminist rhetoric; it's almost as if they don't exist. And perhaps they didn't exist in the lives of these feminists. Perhaps like their broken relationships with their parents, or with husbands and lovers, their relationships with their children were just as strained. But more likely, the absence is to steer their arguments toward their own agenda and away from the richness of authentic, deep, and selfless relationships.

We also have to look at the data that elite feminists don't talk about. Instead of constantly looking for scapegoats and reasons for our victimhood, we need to take responsibility for our own actions and behavior. The time to consider having a child isn't after she is conceived. The time for figuring out if you want to spend the rest of your life with a man isn't after you have been living together for years. We must discuss the needs of children and how much better off they are with their father and mother married to each other and living in one home. We need to discuss the devastating effects of divorce on children, including adult children who carry the wounds of divorce. We need to discuss the complementarity of men and women and what husbands and wives bring to each other, not in an unhealthy way, but in a way where they enrich each other. Women need men and men need women—and children need both parents.

Mother

Louise Perry's book *The Case against the Sexual Revolution* surveys the significant changes that have taken place between women and men since the 1960s. What struck me most about the book was a very short, poignant section that marks the end of the book. Perry explains how a young woman named Abby thought about her life. In her viral TikTok video, Abby made this confession:

> I, like many other college students, am someone who is entangled in hookup culture, and often hookup culture makes it difficult for me to determine whether or not what I'm doing is, you know, good for me and kind to myself. And I think very often, especially as [women], we are led astray from what we genuinely, actually deserve. So here's what I've been doing lately.... [3]

Perry then describes how Abby "pulls up on screen a series of childhood photos of herself and explains that the men she's hooked up with in the past have often made her feel as though she's undeserving, not only of love but also of basic respect. So she's trying to remind herself of her worth as a person by playing the role of mother to her inner child. 'Am I OK with that for her?,' she asks tearfully, gesturing at her younger self in the photo."[4] Abby asks herself: "Would I let this happen to her?

Would I let her be a late-night, drunk second option?...From a third person, caretaker point of view, I would never let any of this stuff happen to her."[5] Perry then offers this incisive summary:

> Abby is trying to mother herself, though she isn't quite sure how to do it. And the thousands of young women in her replies are trying to do the same ("I'm sobbing"; "i rlly needed this, thank you"; "this just changed my life"). They've been denied the guidance of mothers, not because their actual mothers are unwilling to offer it but because of a matricidal impulse in liberal feminism that cuts young women off from the "problematic" older generation. This means not only that they are cut off from the voices of experience, but—more importantly—they are also cut off from the person who loves them most in the world. Feminism needs to rediscover the mother, in every sense.[6]

Yes, we are cut off from mothers, for the reasons Perry enumerates, but also because women have been told to act like men (and bad men at that), to leave the home, and to take care of their own lives to the detriment of their family and loved ones—and to abandon their children without a second thought. Relationships become tenuous, shallow, and strained by lack of time, communication, understanding, presence, and focus. Women have been told that their lives as mothers aren't very important, so many don't put as much into it as they would like, or they don't have the time to give it as much as they wish. Mothers, like everyone else on the planet, only have so much energy for one day. We have been told to spend it on ourselves, or our corporate boss.

There are very few words like "mother." We mourn and weep when a mother dies, sensing the gravity of it, even when it is a mother we don't know. We feel it keenly when a mother isn't who she is supposed to be.

We honor our mothers, but somehow this best of the best has been deemed the worst of the worst. This is what has to change, along with the rhetoric of drudgery and enslavement so common in feminist writing. There must be a shift from the idea that "my children are here to serve me," back to the ancient wisdom that "we are here to serve them." It is only then that the lost get found—the lost girls who are already mothers, and the lost girls and boys who are their daughters and sons.

We also need to rehabilitate the home and the idea of homemaking, which is a funny thing to suggest as nearly every home art has come back into vogue: knitting, bread-baking, gardening, cooking. Of course, not every woman will become a homemaker, but this role needs to be restored as the incredible and important gift we give to our children, that we give to ourselves to mother them, and that we give to our husbands, as a place where our lives are supported and thick relationships are formed. The home isn't meant to be a hotel, where people see each other at night, but an authentic place of memory-building, nurturing, listening, dancing, toasting, praying, resting, and serving. Home is meant to be a place where the family does the work of being a family, forming the immature to go out into the world whole and intact or offering a safe harbor for older family members later in life.

What Is a Woman?

What, then, does it mean to be a woman? The ancient thinkers (and the not-so ancient) have recognized patterns about women. In our confused world, many object and say, *Men can do these things, too*, and to varying degrees they might be right; many activities do cross over. But there is one thing only women can do: give birth to a child. Women give life. Women in some degree have the capacity or potential for this, even if it isn't actualized, or is, for some reason, thwarted. Mothering and motherhood are essential pieces of womanhood. This is what keeps the species alive. It is vital and essential, and up until recently, it was recognized as the most tender and natural of relational bonds. It is one of the strongest of human bonds on earth. There are few things that elicit the strength, courage, patience, perseverance, fortitude, and innovation of a mother's love for her child.

The ancients used the river as a metaphor for women's life-giving capacity. The Nile River has long been called "the mother of all men." Rivers are known as the "cradles of civilizations" because their water brings life to a desert, as in a place like northern Africa. Mother Nature is also considered a she, because nature provides life to all of humanity. These are the things that women do and what women are: they are life-bearers, cradling, nourishing, and moving what will become the future, much of which the woman will never witness herself.

Nourish

Women also nourish their children. The necessity of breastfeeding is overlooked because of the availability of infant formula, but prior to that, women had to have either their own milk or a wet nurse in order for their child to survive. The scarcity of infant formula in 2022 brought this home to many people who had never given it a second thought. The first thing a healthy newborn baby does after breathing is suckle. He is ready to eat. What nourishing women do, of course, isn't limited to breast milk or even to food. Women nourish others in their needs, trying to do the best we can as teachers, mentors, friends, or some other kind of surrogate in giving others what they authentically need.

Holding

In the Romance languages, words like "ocean," "ship," "city," and "oven" are feminine. This is why boats are named after women.[7] Even the Church is considered feminine. The word in Latin for "church" is "ecclesia" a feminine noun. In French "église" is likewise feminine. The Church is nourishing, it gives and cradles life. It is also a place of movement, of change, of transition, from a child's baptism to funerals for the dead.

Women's bodies have the capacity to hold based on the build of our hips, our arms made in a way that naturally cradles a baby, and wombs that are the first home for every human being. But women don't just carry things; we can transform them, change them, improve them. When holding and nurturing come together, the results can be life-changing, life-giving, life-sustaining.

Holding isn't just for biological mothers, but all women. All women are called to hold others in their minds, hearts, prayers, and even in their arms. This is what philosopher Edith Stein meant when she said, "Woman's soul is...fashioned to be a shelter in which other souls unfold."[8] This means that we hold others in our hearts and minds in a way that provides for and protects them, not just from beasts and famine but also from the small stuff.

Women also have the ability to hold together things that we don't normally couple together, like warmth and work, tenderness and tenacity, patience and dynamism. This is not to say that men don't have these abilities, but nothing can provoke the seeming opposites of gentleness and fierceness in a woman like what she loves.

This is a short sketch, with vast room for others to help us understand ourselves better as we emerge from feminism's confines.

The Fly-Over Women

First it was women like Betty and Gloria.
Which gave way to Oprah and Madonna.
Followed by RBG, Hillary, and Ellen.
And now there are Beyoncé, Kamala, and AOC.

It is clear that those who disagree with them don't have nearly the same name recognition, women with names like Sarah Sanders, Amy Coney Barrett, Rachel Duffy, Lila Rose, and Mary Ann Glendon.

There is another litany of names, women unknown to most: Andrea, Rebecca, Joyce, and Leigha, who love, nurture, console, clothe, clean, and adore their children. These are also the women we will never see in the splashy pages of *Vanity Fair*, *Vogue*, or *Architectural Digest*. They represent a category of women in America whom most of us know but who are scarcely represented in the media. They are everyday women, the non-elite, the fabric that holds this country together. These are the 42 percent, pro-life women who don't abide by the elite narrative despite its reach, rejecting abortion and embracing the sanctity of life and marriage.

From Maine to Hawaii, these women have opened themselves up to the dramatic and self-sacrificial love required when one person truly loves another. They carry children in their wombs, their arms, their hearts, their minds. They know the preciousness of a tender embrace from small arms, a little face learning to offer kisses, the peppering of questions from a curious child, and the dig-deep challenges of teenagers—sometimes all in the same hour. Some know the struggle of children with broken bodies, or broken minds, or both. And some know the gaping hole that will never be filled when a child or children are lost. But among them all, there isn't a single regret in bringing another soul into the world.

There are other women, with names like Natalie, Mary, and Gloria Christi, who are single, religious sisters, grandmothers, or women who haven't had children, but who understand deeply the value of spiritual motherhood and the importance of mentoring, loving, and caring for the most vulnerable among us.

Fly-over women are the moms and daughters and wives and sisters and friends the media overlooks because they are religious or don't have sexy day jobs. They are considered uneducated doormats. Their bodies are often tired, hair not always perfectly coiffed, and nails rarely manicured. Their homes may not be camera-ready, their meals probably aren't gourmet, and talking points aren't ready on their tongues. The real issue is that they don't believe in abortion and they do believe in the sanctity of marriage. They don't want to be called "birthing persons," and they know that no amount of hormones will make their sons their daughters or their daughters their sons.

These unseen and unknown women are the fly-over women in every American city and state. They've been called bigots, lectured to, condescended to, and ignored by those who consider themselves morally superior. More than anything, these women actively reject the ideology continually advanced by radical feminism. They are tired of the Marxist effort to reimagine human nature as anything it wants to be. They reject all the latest fads, propagated with clever sound bites, high-end advertising, and popular hashtags.

The fly-over woman understands her womanhood and motherhood deep in her bones and doesn't see maleness as a goal to achieve or a person to conquer. She knows she needs men. She knows, as women have for millennia, that being a woman is synonymous with carrying and nurturing someone.

While HuffPost announced that "child-free women are having a bit of a moment in the media,"[9] one wonders what they think the last fifty years have been. We are living amid a tremendous societal experiment that is revealing dramatically what happens when you denigrate the most fundamental, beautiful, and tender bond on earth—the bond between a mother and child. When that is destroyed, it doesn't take long for the rest of civilization to follow the same path, as we now witness daily.

There are a lot of fly-over women out here. Many of us feel alone, overwhelmed, exhausted, and unseen. But we will continue to raise our families as best we can, however imperfectly, navigating the constant messaging and policies out of step with our own values and beliefs, because we know that without strong families, what's left of civilization will collapse overnight.

Fly-over women know that there are more satisfying ways to live, where dignity is honored, health is valued, body parts aren't ignored or rendered useless, and relationships—close to the heart of most women—aren't fleeting or shallow, useful or convenient, but deep, abiding, and life-giving. Many of us have learned this the hard way, have learned from our scars, and have matured through suffering. We came to the realization that everything that feminism promised did not come to fruition. All the things we thought feminists were doing right didn't lead us to happiness but to an unrecognizable place they never acknowledged.

Like a sleeping giant, these women are waking up and realizing they are not alone anymore. That reality has the dramatic capacity to transform our culture, wherever we work and spend our energies.

Where to from Here?

It is hard for most of us to imagine giving up feminism. Doing so opens our minds to a flood of concerns and anxieties, as change often does. Would we go back to the 1940s? What would take its place? How would we think of our place in culture as women? Wouldn't we just become chattel again? There is something comfortable and comforting about an ideology that we have all been wrapped in—like Linus's blanket—for all of our lives. How would we possibly move forward?

What, then, practically speaking, should we convey to women of every economic and ethnic stripe to help us have fulfilling lives outside of feminism? There are basics, such as, don't sleep around, don't do drugs, don't have abortions, stop blaming the patriarchy, find a purpose outside of yourself, don't overspend, get rid of your *Fifty Shades* books, pray, and figure out what is truly good, not just what celebrities tell you to do and believe. None of these suggestions are revolutionary, especially if one looks honestly at history, human nature, or psychology.

Much of this book has focused on female power. Women are incredibly powerful. Elizabeth Cady Stanton predicted that the women's movement would unleash "the greatest revolution the world has ever seen,"[10] and she was not mistaken, if one means size and influence rather than moral goodness. If we were not powerful, our culture would never have succumbed to the damage wrought by feminism and its "great revolution." The problem is that we haven't used our power properly.

Mallory Millett, Kate Millett's sister, pointed out that most women, when they read of Eve's temptation to eat the fruit from the tree of good and evil in Genesis 3, look at it and believe that women are evil or weak because she succumbed to the temptation. What they miss is the power of Eve. Eve took the fruit, but so did Adam. Eve, in his eyes, was more important than God. He fell because the love he had for Eve eclipsed his love for God. "Adam was willing to defy even God to make this woman happy, just to please this woman," said Mallory. "We have power," she added. "We have incredible power, but we must learn how to use it well."[11] We can see that this is true in the power Meghan Markle has over Prince Harry, as Wallis Simpson had over Prince Harry's great great-uncle before him, King Edward VIII, who abdicated the crown for an American divorcée. These men placed women above their family, country, duty, and honor. Men all over the world and throughout history know this power.

To move forward, women must recognize where our real power lies and understand how to use it well. We must also end the vilification of men and move to restore the family. If we do these things, the world will not come to an end—quite the contrary, like a barren garden, it will emerge slowly, coming back to life, to be reanimated with those elements that we have grasped at but missed.

We can never expect to live in a utopia. There will always be bad men and bad women, because we live in a world where we are given a choice to live according to what we love. But at a certain point, men and women need to abandon their vices and put their faith in God and each other to build a system based on positive, life-building ideals, rather than pursuing a race to the bottom in the battle of the sexes.

It is time for us to come home: to come home and love our children instead of discarding them biologically or emotionally, to come home to husbands and to work with them against a common enemy instead of making them the enemy. And it is time to come home to ourselves, as women and mothers.

If only we could find a way to tell this to every woman. She could choose it or reject it, but at least she would know there is another way to live, to love, and to be made whole.

Acknowledgments

E very book that I write feels like an odyssey, a journey from that place where it is just small spark of an idea, the many days when I'm overwhelmed by the research, fatigued from the fight to "sculpt water" into something intelligible, the scouring of tiny minutiae in endnotes and prose, to a finished product that I can scarcely believe is finished. Like a quest, there is always soul searching, a desire to give up, turn back, scuttle the whole thing. One foot in front of the other is the only way forward.

I never write my books on my own. In fact, I don't think that if I had remained single that I would have ever written books. My remarkable husband has given me the confidence, and my amazing children have given me other virtues, like perseverance, but also patience and a determination to help them to see the truth, even when the rest of the world is screaming the false.

Thanks to Noelle Mering and Alexandra DeSanctis for their diligent and patient reading of my drafts. Thank you also to Ryan Anderson, David and Margaret Bereit, Andrea Picciotti-Bayer, Barbara A. Grasso, Yesi Lemus, Emily Malloy, Kimberly Cook, and Mary A. Nicholas, for your insights and encouragement. Thank you, Mallory Millett, for the support and wisdom you brought to this project. I'm also grateful to Carl Trueman and his triumph of a book, *The Rise and Triumph of the Modern Self*, for shedding light on many of the issues covered in this book.

I'm grateful for everyone at Regnery for believing in this book, especially Tom Spence, who saw the vision, and Anthony Meffe, who, along with Elizabeth Kantor and Joshua Monnington, helped me make it a reality.

And finally, I would like to thank my mother and maternal grandmother, for their gift of life, of love, femininity, their domestic arts and business chops, and the witness of showing me the great lengths to which women will go when they love their families.

Many thanks to the publications who have published articles that were modified and used in this book.[1]

Notes

Epigraph

WordToTheWise, "LOOK WHERE YOU LEAST WANT TO—Powerful Life Advice | Jordan Peterson," YouTube, September 11, 2019, https://www.youtube.com/watch?v=LjIAzKo62MQ. This is an adaptation of Carl Jung's "That which you most need to find will be found where you least want to look."

Introduction: Vulnerability and Patriarchy

1. Barbara Goldsmith, *Other Powers: The Age of Suffrage, Spiritualism, and the Scandalous Victoria Woodhull* (New York: HarperPerennial, 1999), 172–73.
2. *Merriam-Webster*, s.v. "patriarchy (n.)," https://www.merriam-webster.com/dictionary/patriarchy.
3. Sylvia Walby, "Theorising Patriarchy," *Sociology* 23, no. 2 (May 1989): 213–34.
4. Kate Millett, *Sexual Politics* (New York: Ballantine Books, 1970), 33.
5. Ibid.
6. Judith Butler, "Disorderly Woman," Transition, no. 53 (1991): 91, https://doi.org/10.2307/2935175.
7. Charlotte Higgins, "The Age of Patriarchy: How an Unfashionable Idea Became a Rallying Cry for Feminism Today," The Guardian, June 22, 2018, https://www.theguardian.com/news/2018/jun/22/the-age-of-patriarchy-how-an-unfashionable-idea-became-a-rallying-cry-for-feminism-today.
8. Matt Walsh, *What Is a Woman?*, directed and produced by Justin Folk (Nashville, Tennessee: DailyWire+, 2022).
9. Carolyn Downey, "Judge Jackson Refuses to Define 'Woman' during Confirmation Hearing: 'I'm Not a Biologist,'" *National Review*, March 23, 2022, https://www.nationalreview.com/news/judge-jackson-refuses-to-define-woman-during-confirmation-hearing-im-not-a-biologist/. The new "women"—the ones she is trying not to offend—aren't biologically women, so a biology degree wouldn't help her.

10. Gabriella Swerling, "Cambridge Dictionary Updates Definition of 'Woman,'" *The Telegraph*, December 13, 2022, https://www.telegraph.co.uk/news/2022/12/13/cambridge-dictonary-definition-woman-trans-female-update/.

11. Ibid. This version won't last long because it implies that there are still only two genders.

12. Betsey Stevenson and Justin Wolfers, "The Paradox of Declining Female Happiness" (working paper, National Bureau of Economic Research, May 2009), https://www.nber.org/papers/w14969.

13. Ibid.

14. Ibid.

15. Catherine Turvey, "Women More Likely Than Men to Initiate Divorces, but Not Non-Marital Breakups," press release, American Sociological Association, August 22, 2015, https://www.asanet.org/women-more-likely-men-initiate-divorces-not-non-marital-breakups/.

16. Lionel Tiger, *The Decline of Males* (New York: Golden Books, 1999).

17. Mary Kate Cary, "What's Hidden in Obama's 'Julia' Campaign," *U.S. News & World Report*, May 4, 2012, https://www.usnews.com/opinion/blogs/mary-kate-cary/2012/05/04/whats-hidden-in-obamas-julia-campaign.

18. Nidhi Subbaraman, "Homicide Is a Top Cause of Maternal Death in the United States," *Nature*, November 21, 2021, https://www.nature.com/articles/d41586-021-03392-8.

19. Ellipsis in the original. Roxane Gay, *Bad Feminist: Essays* (New York: HarperPerennial, 2014), x–xi.

20. Ibid., xii.

21. Jordan B Peterson, "Modern Times: Camille Paglia & Jordan B. Peterson," YouTube, October 2, 2017, quoted portion begins at 37:20, https://www.youtube.com/watch?v=v-hIVnmUdXM.

Part I: The Lost Girls

1. Phyllis Chesler, *A Politically Incorrect Feminist: Creating a Movement with Bitches, Lunatics, Dykes, Prodigies, Warriors, and Wonder Women* (New York: St. Martin's Press, 2018), chapter 1; Debra Michals, "Gloria Steinem," National Women's History Museum, 2017, www.womenshistory.org/education-resources/biographies/gloria-steinem.

Chapter 1: Mary, the First Feminist

1. So well-known is her patriarchy-smashing commitment that she was given an original drawing featuring her rescue pup, Guy, toppling the patriarchy.

It reads, "Who's a good boy? Who's a good boy?" with the dog responding, "A boy who makes an effort to dismantle the patriarchy whilst keeping in mind intersections with other forms of oppression." Zoe Weiner, "Someone Gave Meghan Markle a Drawing of Her Dog Toppling the Patriarchy," *Glamour*, October 3, 2018, https://www.glamour.com/story/meghan-markle -drawing-dog-patriarchy.

2. "Prince Harry Says 'Megxit' Is a Misogynistic Term Aimed at His Wife Meghan," *The Guardian*, November 9, 2021, https://www.theguardian.com /uk-news/2021/nov/10/prince-harry-says-megxit-is-a-misogynistic-term -aimed-at-his-wife-meghan.

3. Allison P. Davis, "Meghan of Montecito," The Cut, August 29, 2022, https:// www.thecut.com/article/meghan-markle-profile-interview.html.

4. Ibid.

5. Maximilien Robespierre, "Robespierre's Speech of February 5, 1794," in *Major Crises in Western Civilization*, ed. Richard W. Lyman and Lewis W. Spitz, vol. 2, *1745 to the Nuclear Age* (New York: Harcourt, Brace & World, 1965), 71–72.

6. The Romantics during this period tried to re-use virtue from the ancient Greek period because it didn't have any associations with Christianity, but they also disassociated it from the important elements like the *polis*, or city, and by extension the family, tradition, and duty, so it was a very narrow use of the word virtue.

7. Charlotte Gordon, *Romantic Outlaws: The Extraordinary Lives of Mary Wollstonecraft and Her Daughter Mary Shelley* (New York: Random House, 2015), 15.

8. William Godwin, *Memoirs of the Author of "A Vindication of The Rights of Woman"* (London, 1798), 7.

9. Ibid., 2.

10. Mary Wollstonecraft, *A Vindication of the Rights of Men* (London, 1790), 119–20, https://oll.libertyfund.org/title/wollstonecraft-a-vindication-of-the -rights-of-men.

11. Godwin, *Memoirs of the Author*, 94.

12. William Godwin, *Enquiry Concerning Political Justice*, 3rd ed. (London, 1798), 508.

13. Godwin was among the many critics of her writing style—thinking it undisciplined. Mary would respond by citing her Romantic roots and claiming it as spontaneous and full of feeling and emotion, Romantic ideals.

14. Queer theorist Judith Butler won the Bad Writing Contest for philosophy and literature in 1998 for this gem: "The move from a structuralist account in which capital is understood to structure social relations in relatively homologous ways to a view of hegemony in which power relations are subject to repetition, convergence, and rearticulation brought the question of temporality into the thinking of structure, and marked a shift from a form of Althusserian theory that takes structural totalities as theoretical objects to one in which the insights into the contingent possibility of structure inaugurate a renewed conception of hegemony as bound up with the contingent sites and strategies of the rearticulation of power." "The World's Worst Writing," *The Guardian*, December 24, 1999, https://www.theguardian.com/books/1999/dec/24/news.

15. Mary Wollstonecraft, *A Vindication of the Rights of Woman* (Boston, 1792), 35.

16. Ibid., 36–37.

17. Ibid., 19.

18. "What Was Thomas Paine's Stance on Women's Rights?," The Thomas Paine Historical Society, 2023, https://thomaspaine.org/pages/resources/what-was-thomas-paine-s-stance-on-women-s-rights.html.

19. Wollstonecraft, *Vindication of the Rights of Woman*, 18.

20. Ibid., 43.

21. Ibid., chapter 1.

22. Ibid., 34.

23. Maximilien Robespierre, *On the Principles of Political Morality Which Are to Form the Basis of the Administration of the Interior Concerns of the Republic* (Philadelphia, 1794), https://www.marxists.org/history/france/revolution/robespierre/1794/political-morality.htm.

24. Although the Enlightenment idea of virtue seemed to be calling forth the same notion of virtue as the ancient Greeks, it was actually quite different because of both theological and rational differences between the ages.

25. Wollstonecraft, *Vindication of the Rights of Woman*, 22.

26. Ibid., 18.

27. Sarah Trimmer to Mrs. M., July 12, 1792, in *Some Account of the Life and Writings of Mrs. Trimmer, with Original Letters, and Mediations and Prayers, Selected from her Journal* (London, 1814), 2:354–55.

28. At one point she fell in love with an older married gentleman and suggested that she move in with the couple. The wife refused, horrified by the suggestion, and Mary left town, biographers suggest, because she was embarrassed by

Notes
195

the situation. Gordon, *Romantic Outlaws*, 180–82; Godwin, *Memoirs of the Author*, 33.

Chapter 2: Mary and the Romantics

1. "Satan's Teen Daughter," FX, https://www.fxnetworks.com/shows/little -demon.

2. Benjamin Fearnow, "Number of Witches Rise Dramatically across U.S. as Millennials Reject Christianity," *Newsweek*, November 18, 2018, https:// www.newsweek.com/witchcraft-wiccans-mysticism-astrology-witches -millennials-pagans-religion-1221019.

3. Madonna (@Madonna), "The Patriarchy continues to crush...," Twitter, February 19, 2021, 8:18 p.m., https://twitter.com/madonna/status /1362934554647003137?lang=en.

4. Thomas D. Williams, "Madonna Mocks Christ's Last Supper in Vanity Fair Photo Shoot," Breitbart, January 23, 2023, https://www.breitbart.com /entertainment/2023/01/23/madonna-mocks-christs-last-supper-in-vanity -fair-photo-shoot/.

5. Richard Holmes, *Shelley: The Pursuit* (London: Flamingo, 1995), x.

6. Charlotte Gordon, *Romantic Outlaws: The Extraordinary Lives of Mary Wollstonecraft and Her Daughter Mary Shelley* (New York: Random House, 2015), 85–86.

7. Per Faxneld, *Satanic Feminism: Lucifer as the Liberator of Women in Nineteenth-Century Culture* (New York: Oxford University Press, 2017), 77. Also noted here is Mary Wollstonecraft's mention of Satan in a footnote of *A Vindication of Rights of Women*. She tells "of her dislike for scenes of 'paradisiacal happiness' where Milton depicts the marital bliss of Adam and Eve and instead 'with conscious dignity, or satanic pride', turns to hell for sublimer subjects.'"

8. Ibid., 79.

9. John Milton, *Paradise Lost*, book 1, 263.

10. Ibid., book 4, 70.

11. Ibid., book 4, 110.

12. Faxneld, *Satanic Feminism*, 82.

13. "With Genesis 3, we turn to what is perhaps one of the momentous chapters in the Old Testament: the account of the Fall. With this narrative, Genesis reveals to us the sin that lay at the origins of mankind and, therefore, the root cause of all moral evils with which human history has been inundated...."

"A general theme of chapter 3 is the *inversion of norms*. Everything is turned upside down. In the divinely established order in Genesis 1–2, Adam, God's vice-regent, is to obey God. He is to communicate God's will to Eve, his spouse, and together they are to rule over the animals. In the course of Genesis 3, the animal (the serpent) is going to rule over Eve, Eve is going to communicate the animal's will to Adam, and together all three will defy God." John Bergsma and Brant Pitre, *A Catholic Introduction to the Bible: The Old Testament* (San Francisco: Ignatius Press, 2018), 105.

14. Faxneld, *Satanic Feminism*, 82.

15. Ibid., 81.

16. Ibid., 83.

17. Ibid.

18. Ibid.

19. Ibid., 83–84. Here again, Shelley uses virtue in the same way Wollstonecraft did.

20. Ellipsis Faxneld's. Ibid., 83.

21. Ibid., 84.

22. Ibid.

23. Percy Bysshe Shelley to Elizabeth Hitchener, November 16, 1811, in *The Complete Works of Percy Bysshe Shelley*, ed. Roger Ingpen and Walter E. Peck (New York: Gordian Press, 1965), 8:205.

24. For a fuller treatment of de Sade's influence on Shelley, see Susan Miller, "Shelley's Early Fiction in Relation to His Poetics and his Politics: An Assessment" (Ph.D. thesis, University of Glasgow, 2013), https://theses.gla .ac.uk/4130/1/2012millerphd.pdf.

25. Guillaume Apollinaire, *Les Diables Amoureux* (Paris: Gallimard, 1964), quoted in Miller, "Shelley's Early Fiction," 31.

26. Anne Williams, "'Mummy, Possest': Sadism and Sensibility in Shelley's *Frankenstein*," Romantic Circles, July 2003, https://romantic-circles.org /praxis/frankenstein/williams/williams.html.

27. Holmes, *Shelley*, ix.

28. Ellipses Gordon's. Gordon, *Romantic Outlaws*, 522–23.

29. Ibid., xvii.

30. Ibid., 81.

31. Ibid., 306.

32. Ibid., 435–36.

33. Ellipses Hay's. This is a quote found in newly discovered letters written by Claire Clairmont first published in Daisy Hay, *Young Romantics: The*

Tangled Lives of English Poetry's Greatest Generation (New York: Farrar, Straus and Giroux, 2010), 308.

34. Ben Downing, "Love's Pestilence," *New York Times*, July 9, 2010, https://www.nytimes.com/2010/07/11/books/review/Downing-t.html.

35. Friedrich Nietzsche, *The Gay Science*, trans. Thomas Common (Mineola, New York: Dover Publications, Inc., 2006), 90–91.

Chapter 3: Elizabeth and Seneca's Fall

1. The term feminism wouldn't be used until the 1880s, first in France.

2. Judith Wellman, *The Road to Seneca Falls: Elizabeth Cady Stanton and the First Woman's Rights Convention* (Urbana and Chicago: University of Illinois, 2004), 11.

3. Susan B. Anthony was written into Stanton's history of Seneca Falls after the fact, as the two women would not meet until three years after the event.

4. Barbara Goldsmith, *Other Powers: The Age of Suffrage, Spiritualism, and the Scandalous Victoria Woodhull* (New York: HarperPerennial, 1999), xiii.

5. Ibid., 150.

6. Wellman, *Road to Seneca Falls*, 19.

7. Ibid., 27.

8. Ibid., 161.

9. Ibid.

10. Ibid., 162.

11. Eleanor Flexner and Ellen Fitzpatrick, *Century of Struggle: The Woman's Rights Movement in the United States*, enlarged ed. (Cambridge, Massachusetts: Belknap Press, 1996), 68.

12. Wellman, *Road to Seneca Falls*, 32.

13. Goldsmith, *Other Powers*, 45.

14. Hal D. Sears, *The Sex Radicals: Free Love in High Victorian America* (Lawrence, Kansas: Regents Press of Kansas, 1977), 36.

15. Ibid., 8.

16. Ibid., 22.

17. Even as late as 1905, free love adherents were inspired by Wollstonecraft, Godwin, and Shelley. "The 'sex cranks' of the Comstock era, however, drew ideas from a surprising range of thinkers. One essayist in 1905 acknowledged not only Mary Wollstonecraft, William Godwin, and the poet Shelley . . ." Ibid., 25.

18. Goldsmith, *Other Powers*, 49.

19. Sears, *Sex Radicals*, 6–7.

20. Ibid.

21. Wellman, *Road to Seneca Falls*, 219. Even Susan B. Anthony was a believer in the rapping. Stanton was the brain and Anthony became the voice of their effort, although Anthony was not well suited to public speaking. "Even she sought help from spiritual sources. While on the road she wrote to Stanton, 'Oh dear, dear! If the *spirits* would only just make me a *trance medium* and put the *rights* into my mouth. You can't think how earnestly I have prayed to be made a speaking medium for a whole week. If they would only come to me thus, I'd give them a hearty welcome.'" Goldsmith, *Other Powers*, 48.

22. Goldsmith, *Other Powers*, 48.

23. Brackets and ellipses Goldsmith's. Ibid.

24. First ellipsis added. Ibid., 38.

25. Emphasis and ellipsis in the original. Ibid., 38–39.

26. Wellman, *Road to Seneca Falls*, 192.

27. Ibid.

28. Ibid., 193.

29. Ibid., 10.

30. Per Faxneld, *Satanic Feminism: Lucifer as the Liberator of Women in Nineteenth-Century Culture* (New York: Oxford University Press, 2017), 130.

31. Gloria Steinem, *Revolution from Within: A Book of Self-Esteem* (New York: Open Road Media, 2012), 65, Kindle.

32. Faxneld, *Satanic Feminism*, 109.

33. Ibid., 125.

34. Elizabeth Cady Stanton, *The Woman's Bible*, 2 vols. (New York: Rainbow Classics, 2016), 17, Kindle.

35. Ibid., 18.

36. Faxneld, *Satanic Feminism*, 135.

37. Kathi Kern, *Mrs. Stanton's Bible* (Ithaca, New York: Cornell University Press, 2001), 177, quoted in Faxneld, *Satanic Feminism*, 137.

38. Faxneld, *Satanic Feminism*, 137.

39. Sears, *Sex Radicals*, 5.

40. Brackets and ellipsis Lemay's. Kate Clark Lemay, *Votes for Women* (Washington, D.C.: National Portrait Gallery, 2019), 10–11.

41. Allison Lange, "Suffragists Organize: American Woman Suffrage Association," National Women's History Museum, 2015, http://www.crusadeforthevote.org/awsa-organize.

42. Goldsmith, *Other Powers*, 272.

43. Brackets Goldsmith's. Ibid., xi, xiv, 3, 7.
44. Ibid., xiv.
45. Victoria made it clear that she knew the details of the lurid affair and others carried out by men associated with the AWSA who had renounced her. Initially, in an effort to prevent her from publishing the scandal, Tilton charmed her and the two ended up lovers. Beecher caved to Victoria's financial demands to keep her silence, but eventually, all the charm and money meant to silence her wasn't enough, and Victoria went rogue, publishing all the salacious details of Beecher's affair with Lib Tilton.
46. Goldsmith, *Other Powers*, 230–31.
47. Ibid., 435.

Chapter 4: Betty and the Communist Mystique

1. Eleanor Flexner and Ellen Fitzpatrick, *Century of Struggle: The Woman's Rights Movement in the United States*, enlarged ed. (Cambridge, Massachusetts: Belknap Press, 1996), 85.
2. Marx was a follower of Rousseau, but also believed that William Godwin's work *Political Justice* made him an icon of revolution. Both Marx and Engels "took up Godwin as their hero, citing him as an important influence." Charlotte Gordon, *Romantic Outlaws: The Extraordinary Lives of Mary Wollstonecraft and Her Daughter Mary Shelley* (New York: Random House, 2015), 361.
3. Bill Keller, "Major Soviet Paper Says 20 Million Died as Victims of Stalin," *New York Times*, February 4, 1989, https://www.nytimes.com/1989/02/04/world/major-soviet-paper-says-20-million-died-as-victims-of-stalin.html.
4. Whittaker Chambers, *Witness,* 50th anniversary ed. (Washington, D.C.: Regnery Gateway, 1980), 16.
5. Mary Nichols and Paul Kengor, *The Devil and Bella Dodd: One Woman's Struggle against Communism and Her Redemption* (Gastonia, North Carolina: TAN Books, 2022), 2.
6. Bella Dodd, *School of Darkness* (New York: Devin-Adair Company, 1954), 194–95.
7. Committee on Un-American Activities: U.S. House of Representatives, *Report on the Congress of American Women* (Washington, D.C.: U.S. Government Printing Office, 1950), 16, quoting *Soviet Woman*, no. 1, 1946, (January–February), 10.
   My favorite bit of propaganda was from this article, "New Vistas Open to the Women of New Russia," by Walter Duranty for the *New York Times*,

where he discusses how virtuous women in the Soviet Union are because they are no longer frequenting hair salons. Walter Duranty, "New Vistas Open to the Women of New Russia," *New York Times*, March 15, 1936. Of course, the reality is, they probably could no longer afford hair salons, but that didn't make it into the piece. Walter Duranty had been instrumental in covering up the extent of the Soviet-engineered famine in Ukraine in the '30s, today known as the Holodomor, so he was no stranger to putting a bright spin on devastation.

8. Flexner, who wrote *Century of Struggle* in 1959, "the first scholarly history of American women and a virtual bible for the 1960s feminist, is another figure whose career links radicalism beginning in the 1930s with post-1960 feminism. In 1983 Flexner sent boxes of her papers to the Schlesinger Library. They contained copies of articles she wrote for the *Daily Worker*, evidence of her involvement with the Communist Party." Daniel Horowitz, *Betty Friedan and the Making of the Feminine Mystique: The American Left, the Cold War, and Modern Feminism* (Amherst: University of Massachusetts Press, 1998), 125.

9. Charlotte Higgins, "The Age of Patriarchy: How an Unfashionable Idea Became a Rallying Cry for Feminists Today," *The Guardian*, June 22, 2018, https://www.theguardian.com/news/2018/jun/22/the-age-of-patriarchy-how-an-unfashionable-idea-became-a-rallying-cry-for-feminism-today.

10. Ibid.

11. Friedrich Engels, *The Origin of the Family, Private Property, and the State* (New York: Penguin Classics, 2010), 10, Kindle.

Virginia Woolf brought the term into more common parlance with its use in her novel *Three Guineas* (1938). "For her, it described the dynamics within families like hers—in which the father held economic power and authority, boys were trained for public life and girls were debarred from either a serious education or the opportunity to earn a living. The battle lines were drawn 'between the victims of the patriarchal system and the patriarchs.' In other words, it was 'the daughters against the fathers.'" Woolf, however, was more interested in seeing women accrue wealth, believing they could go "from being the victims of the patriarchal system…to being the champions of the capitalist system [ellipsis Higgins's]." Higgins, "Age of Patriarchy."

In 1949 Simone de Beauvoir, who was much more sympathetic to Marx, used "patriarchy" liberally in her book *The Second Sex*. "History has shown," she writes, "that men have always held all the concrete powers; from patriarchy's earliest times they have deemed it useful to keep woman in a state of dependence." Simone de Beauvoir, *The Second Sex* (New York: Vintage Books, 2010), 159, Kindle.

12. Per Faxneld, *Satanic Feminism: Lucifer as the Liberator of Women in Nineteenth-Century Culture* (New York: Oxford University Press, 2017), 103; Hal D. Sears, *The Sex Radicals: Free Love in High Victorian America* (Lawrence, Kansas: Regents Press of Kansas, 1977), 148, 246.

13. Sears, *Sex Radicals*, 25.

14. Kate Weigand, *Red Feminism: American Communism and the Making of Women's Liberation* (Baltimore: Johns Hopkins University Press, 2001), 29.

15. Horowitz, *Betty Friedan*, 7.

16. Ibid.

17. When Friedan's father died, there is no mention of whether her mother was finally happy because she could go back to work.

18. Phyllis Chesler later described her this way: "Betty deserved to be honored, warts and all. Like many of the men who changed history, she was difficult: cantankerous, abusive, abrasive, outrageously demanding—and an out-of-control drunk." Phyllis Chesler, *A Politically Incorrect Feminist: Creating a Movement with Bitches, Lunatics, Dykes, Prodigies, Warriors, and Wonder Women* (New York: St. Martin's Press, 2018), 142.

19. Horowitz, *Betty Friedan*, 69.

20. Ibid., 133.

21. Ibid., 92.

22. Betty Friedan, "Girl Worker Finds Revolt Cooking in U.S. Kitchens," *Fisher Eye Opener* (Cleveland), undated, quoted in Horowitz, *Betty Friedan*, 108.

23. Betty Friedan, *The Feminine Mystique*, 50th anniversary ed. (New York: W. W. Norton & Company, 2013), 243. Amusingly, Gloria Steinem would not hold the line on Friedan's dismissal of bourgeois spending habits. Years later, in her own book, Steinem spoke of the joy she had in finally shopping for a home: "After months of nesting—and shopping for such things as sheets and candles with a pleasure that bordered on orgasmic . . ." Gloria Steinem, *My Life on the Road* (New York: Random House, 2015), 250.

24. Friedan, *Feminine Mystique*, 245.

25. Dodd, *School of Darkness*, 194–95.

26. Horowitz, *Betty Friedan*, 201.

27. Ibid. While the communist message for women was being spread worldwide, curiously, the message of liberating women didn't excite women in China like it did women in the United States. Women who had been homemakers were strongly encouraged to get out of the home and go work in the fields, feeling

their own liberation. However, they didn't quite see it that way. They just knew that they needed to spend the whole day in the fields, doing back-breaking work, and then go home and do all the work at night that they usually had all day to do. There was very little that was attractive to them. The women's movement messaging/propaganda didn't take hold until the "Cultural Revolution" happened in China, where the communists used force to instill these communist ideals.

28. Friedan, *Feminine Mystique*, 276.

29. The subtitle of chapter 12 in *The Feminine Mystique*.

30. Simone de Beauvoir and Betty Friedan, "Sex, Society, and the Female Dilemma: A Dialogue between Simone de Beauvoir and Betty Friedan," *Saturday Review*, June 14, 1975, 18.

31. Horowitz, *Betty Friedan*, 225.

32. See, e.g., Marylin Bender, "Some Call Her the 'Karl Marx' of New Feminism," *New York Times*, July 20, 1970, https://www.nytimes.com/1970/07/20/archives/some-call-her-the-karl-marx-of-new-feminism.html.

Chapter 5: Kate and the Lost Girls' Triumph

1. I have quoted only the participants' words, omitting the repetitive attributions: "they answered," "she replied," "they chanted," and the like. Mallory Millett, "Marxist Feminism's Ruined Lives," FrontPage Magazine, September 1, 2014, https://www.frontpagemag.com/marxist-feminisms-ruined-lives-mallory-millett/.

2. See, e.g., Marylin Bender, "Some Call Her the 'Karl Marx' of New Feminism," *New York Times*, July 20, 1970, https://www.nytimes.com/1970/07/20/archives/some-call-her-the-karl-marx-of-new-feminism.html; Emily Langer, "Kate Millett, 'High Priestess' of Second-Wave Feminism, Dies at 82," *Washington Post*, September 7, 2017, https://www.washingtonpost.com/local/obituaries/kate-millett-high-priestess-of-second-wave-feminism-dies-at-82/2017/09/07/1ccfa2b6-93d4-11e7-aace-04b862b2b3f3_story.html.

3. Herbert Marcuse, *The Aesthetic Dimension: Toward a Critique of Marxist Aesthetics* (Boston: Beacon Press, 1978), 32.

4. Wilhelm Reich, *The Sexual Revolution: Toward a Self-Regulating Character Structure*, trans. Therese Pol (New York: Farrar, Straus and Giroux, 1974), cited in Carl Trueman, *The Rise and Triumph of the Modern Self: Cultural*

Amnesia, Expressive Individualism, and the Road to Sexual Revolution (Wheaton: Crossway, 2020), 236.

5. Reich, *Sexual Revolution*, 25.
6. Trueman, *Rise and Triumph*, 237.
7. See Reich, *Sexual Revolution*, 23 and chapter 14.
8. Parul Sehgal and Neil Genzlinger, "Kate Millett, Ground-Breaking Feminist Writer, Is Dead at 82," *New York Times*, September 6, 2017, https://www.nytimes.com/2017/09/06/obituaries/kate-millett-influential-feminist-writer-is-dead-at-82.html.
9. Mallory Millett, private conversation with the author, December 17, 2022; Millett, "Marxist Feminism's Ruined Lives."
10. Kate Millett, *Sexual Politics* (New York: Ballantine Books, 1970), 33.
11. Charlotte Higgins, "The Age of Patriarchy: How an Unfashionable Idea Became a Rallying Cry for Feminists Today," *The Guardian*, June 22, 2018, https://www.theguardian.com/news/2018/jun/22/the-age-of-patriarchy-how-an-unfashionable-idea-became-a-rallying-cry-for-feminism-today.
12. Millett, *Sexual Politics*, 45.
13. Ibid., 237–38.
14. Martha Shelley, "Notes of a Radical Lesbian," in *Sisterhood is Powerful: An Anthology of Writings from the Women's Liberation Movement*, ed. Robin Morgan (New York: Vintage Books, 1970), 344. "Robin's first anthology, published in 1970, was titled Sisterhood Is Powerful. Forever after, feminists, journalists, and even scholars assumed that the title was a phrase Robin coined. In fact, Kathie Sarachild coined the phrase at a demonstration against the war in Vietnam on January 15, 1968. What kind of sisterhood fails to attribute to its true author a phrase that becomes so popular?" Phyllis Chesler, *A Politically Incorrect Feminist: Creating a Movement with Bitches, Lunatics, Dykes, Prodigies, Warriors, and Wonder Women* (New York: St. Martin's Press, 2018), 215.
15. Shulamith Firestone, *The Dialectic of Sex: The Case for Feminist Revolution* (London: Paladin, 1972), 19.
16. Robin Morgan, ed., *Sisterhood is Powerful: An Anthology of Writings from the Women's Liberation Movement* (New York: Vintage Books, 1970), 538.
17. Chesler, *Politically Incorrect Feminist*, 126.
18. Ibid., 191.
19. Ibid.
20. Ibid., 5.
21. Ibid., 70.

22. Ibid., 5.

23. Ibid., 14.

24. Susan Faludi, "Death of a Revolutionary," *New Yorker*, April 8, 2013.

25. Andrea Dworkin, *Intercourse* (New York: Basic Books, 2007), 3.

26. Valerie Solanas, "Excerpts from the SCUM (Society for Cutting Up Men) Manifesto," in *Sisterhood is Powerful: An Anthology of Writings from the Women's Liberation Movement*, ed. Robin Morgan (New York: Vintage Books, 1970), 514.

27. Ibid., 519.

28. Chesler, *Politically Incorrect Feminist*, 42.

29. Ibid.

30. Suzanne Lucas, "HuffPost Editor Says New Year's Resolution Is to 'Kill All Men,'" Inc., January 2, 2018, https://www.inc.com/suzanne-lucas/huffpost-editor-says-new-years-resolution-is-to-kill-all-men.html.

31. Chesler, *Politically Incorrect Feminist*, 70; Julie Bindel, "Kate Millett Obituary," *The Guardian*, September 7, 2017, https://www.theguardian.com/world/2017/sep/07/kate-millett-obituary; Alice Shalvi, "Andrea Dworkin," *Shalvi/Hyman Encyclopedia of Jewish Women*, December 31, 1999, https://jwa.org/encyclopedia/article/dworkin-andrea.

32. Chesler, *Politically Incorrect Feminist*, 242.

33. Spencer Bright, "Come into My Parlour," *Vox*, February 1992, http://web.archive.org/web/20220626123355/https://fleetwoodmac-uk.com/wp/come-into-my-parlour-vox-magazine-feb-1992/.

34. Ibid.

35. Ibid.

36. For the "Shout Your Abortion" campaign, see Cheryl K. Chumley, "Oprah Winfrey's Despicable 'ShoutYourAbortion' Advocacy," *Washington Times*, August 22, 2018, https://www.washingtontimes.com/news/2018/aug/22/oprah-winfreys-despicable-shoutyourabortion-advoca/; Janet Morana, "Oprah Champions #ShoutYourAbortion and Ignores Women Who Regret Their Abortions," *Washington Examiner*, August 23, 2018, https://www.washingtonexaminer.com/opinion/oprah-champions-shoutyourabortion-and-ignores-women-who-regret-their-abortions. For celebrity abortions, see Li Cohen, "Michelle Williams Advocates for Abortion Rights in Golden Globes Acceptance Speech," CBS News, January 6, 2020, https://www.cbsnews.com/news/golden-globes-michelle-williams-advocates-for-womens-rights-in-golden-globes-speech/; Vanessa Etienne, "Jennifer Grey Details Life-Changing Abortion, Says She's 'Heartbroken' after End of 'Roe v.

Wade,'" *People*, July 14, 2022, https://people.com/health/jennifer-grey
-details-life-changing-abortion-says-shes-heartbroken-after-end-of-roe
-v-wade/; Cydney Henderson, "Alyssa Milano Reveals She Had Two
Abortions in 1993 within Months: 'It Was My Choice,'" *USA TODAY*,
August 20, 2019, https://www.usatoday.com/story/entertainment/celebrities
/2019/08/19/alyssa-milano-reveals-she-had-two-abortions-within-months
-1993/2057829001/; Li Cohen, "Uma Thurman Reveals She Had an Abortion
as a Teenager in Op-Ed Criticizing Texas Law: 'I Have No Regrets,'" CBS
News, September 22, 2021, https://www.cbsnews.com/news/uma-thurman-
abortion-teenager-op-ed-texas-law/; Matt Wilstein, "Chelsea Handler: My
3 Abortions Are Why America Needs Roe," The Daily Beast, June 27, 2022,
https://www.thedailybeast.com/chelsea-handler-says-her-3-abortions-are-
why-america-needs-roe-on-jimmy-kimmel-live; Alex Holder, "11 Powerful
Women Who Have Spoken Out about Their Own Abortion," *Elle*, May 3,
2017, https://www.elle.com/uk/life-and-culture/culture/articles/a33301/10-
powerful-women-who-have-spoken-about-their-own-abortion/.

37. @pappagoblin TikTok video, quoted in Abby Johnson (@prolifeabbyjohnson),
"Cupcakes and Cocktails for Her Abortion," Instagram, October 26, 2022,
https://www.instagram.com/p/CkLgrU5DNq4/.

Chapter 6: Gloria and Selling Feminism

1. Edward Bernays, *Propaganda* (Brooklyn: Ig Publishing, 2004), 1.
2. Ibid., 33.
3. Ibid., 86.
4. Allan M. Brandt, "Recruiting Women Smokers: The Engineering of Consent," *Journal of the American Medical Women's Association* 51, no. 1–2 (1996): 63–66.
5. Gloria Steinem, *Moving Beyond Words* (New York: Simon & Schuster, 1994), 171.
6. Ibid., 173–75.
7. Sarah Halzack, "Lands' End Put Gloria Steinem in Its Catalog. Then It Got an Earful from Customers," *Washington Post*, February 26, 2016, https://www.washingtonpost.com/news/business/wp/2016/02/26/lands-end-put-gloria-steinem-in-its-catalog-then-it-got-an-earful-from-customers/.
8. "Gloria Steinem, the Duchess of Sussex, and Jessica Yellin on Abortion Rights, the ERA, and Why They Won't Give Up Hope," *Vogue*, June 28, 2022, https://www.vogue.com/article/gloria-steinem-duchess-of-sussex-jessica-yellin-roe-v-wade.

9. Amanda Whiting, "Gloria Steinem & Betty Friedan's Friendship Was as Messy as It Looks on 'Mrs. America,'" Bustle, April 21, 2020, https://www.bustle.com/p/gloria-steinem-betty-friedans-complex-relationship-takes-center-stage-in-mrs-america-22834996; Sally Quinn, "Once Again, Feminists Take Up Fight We Shouldn't Have," *Washington Post*, March 14, 2013, https://www.washingtonpost.com/lifestyle/style/once-again-feminists-take-up-fight-we-shouldnt-have/2013/03/14/bed436cc-8ce4-11e2-9f54-f3fdd70acad2_story.html.

10. Phyllis Chesler, *A Politically Incorrect Feminist: Creating a Movement with Bitches, Lunatics, Dykes, Prodigies, Warriors, and Wonder Women* (New York: St. Martin's Press, 2018), 225.

11. Ibid., 227.

12. Karen Brill, "Cate Blanchett Locates Her Moral Compass in Her Vagina," *Vanity Fair*, March 8, 2017, https://www.vanityfair.com/style/2017/03/cate-blanchett-moral-compass-in-vagina.

13. Lilian Faderman, *The Gay Revolution: The Story of the Struggle* (New York: Simon & Schuster, 2015), 218; Eleanor Blau, "Women's G.O.P. Club Honors Foe of ERA," *New York Times*, April 17, 1977.

14. Joyce F. Benenson with Henry Markovitz, *Warriors and Worriers: The Survival of the Sexes* (New York: Oxford University Press, 2014), 130.

15. Ibid., 135.

16. Mary Louise Kelly, Mallory Yu, and Courtney Dorning, "Activist Gloria Steinem Reflects on Abortion Rights as They Hang in the Balance," NPR, December 9, 2021, https://www.npr.org/2021/12/09/1062791724/activist-gloria-steinem-reflects-on-abortion-rights-as-they-hang-in-the-balance.

17. David Ramos, "Feminist Leader Admits 'We Inflated the Figures' to Get Abortion Legalized in Mexico," *Catholic World Report*, September 13, 2022, https://www.catholicworldreport.com/2022/09/13/feminist-leader-admits-we-inflated-the-figures-to-get-abortion-legalized-in-mexico/.

18. Brian Clowes, "Does Legalizing Abortion Stop Filthy, Back-Alley Abortions?," Human Life International, March 4, 2022, https://www.hli.org/resources/doesnt-legal-abortion-save-women-filthy-back-alley-abortion-mills/.

19. Leah Rodriguez, "Gloria Steinem Wants Women to Be Able to Do 'Anything They F*king Well Please,'" Global Citizen, June 8, 2022, https://www.globalcitizen.org/en/content/gloria-steinem-roe-v-wade-abortion-quotes-gc-now/.

20. See the work of Dr. Joel Brind, among others, on the abortion and breast cancer connection. Joel Brind, "Abortion–Breast Cancer Link Explodes in

Asia," Heartbeat International, 2013, https://www.heartbeatinternational
.org/abortion-breast-cancer-link-explodes-in-asia; Joel Brind, "Update on
the Abortion–Breast Cancer Link: Lessons Learned from Asia," Care Net,
https://www.care-net.org/abundant-life-blog/update-on-the-abortion-breast
-cancer-link-lessons-learned-from-asia.

21. Benenson, *Warriors and Worriers*, 185.
22. *Unplanned*, written and directed by Cary Solomon and Chuck Konzelman
(Scottsdale, Arizona: Pure Flix Entertainment, 2019).
23. Gloria Steinem, *Revolution from Within: A Book of Self-Esteem* (Boston:
Little, Brown and Company, 1993), 22–25.

Chapter 7: The Queen Bees and Power

1. Sarah Al-Arshani, "'Women Belong in All Places Where Decisions Are Being
Made. It Shouldn't Be That Women Are the Exception,'" Insider, September
18, 2020, https://www.insider.com/ruth-bader-ginsburgs-memorable-quotes
-throughout-her-life-and-career-2020-9.
2. Ibid.
3. Ibid.
4. Philip Galanes, "Ruth Bader Ginsburg and Gloria Steinem on the Unending
Fight for Women's Rights," *New York Times*, November 14, 2015, https://
www.nytimes.com/2015/11/15/fashion/ruth-bader-ginsburg-and-gloria
-steinem-on-the-unending-fight-for-womens-rights.html.
5. "My Mother Told Me to Be a Lady," AZ Quotes, https://www.azquotes.
com/quote/661440.
6. Cecila Harvey, "When Queen Bees Attack Women Stop Advancing:
Recognising and Addressing Female Bullying in the Workplace,"
Development and Learning in Organizations 32, no. 5 (2018): 1–4, https://
doi.org/10.1108/DLO-04-2018-004.
7. Spencer Brown, "Rep. Maxine Waters Tells Homeless to 'Go Home,'"
Townhall, March 31, 2022, https://townhall.com/tipsheet/spencerbrown
/2022/03/31/go-home-maxine-waters-tells-homeless-people-n2605335.
8. Ella Nilsen, "New Evidence Has Emerged Elizabeth Warren Claimed
American Indian Heritage in 1986," Vox, February 5, 2019, https://www
.vox.com/2018/10/16/17983250/elizabeth-warren-bar-application-american
-indian-dna.
9. Marguerite Bowling, "Video of the Week: 'We Have to Pass the Bill So You
Can Find Out What Is in It," The Daily Signal, March 10, 2010, https://www

.dailysignal.com/2010/03/10/video-of-the-week-we-have-to-pass-the-bill-so -you-can-find-out-what-is-in-it/.

10. Olga Khazan, "Why Do Women Bully Each Other at Work?" *The Atlantic*, September 2017, https://www.theatlantic.com/magazine/archive/2017/09/ the-queen-bee-in-the-corner-office/534213/.

11. Liz Elting, "In Dialogue: Alexis McGill Johnson, President and CEO of Planned Parenthood, on the Future of Reproductive Rights," Forbes, June 14, 2022, https://www.forbes.com/sites/lizelting/2022/06/14/in-dialogue-alexis-mcgill-johnson-president-and-ceo-of-planned-parenthood-on-the-future-of-reproductive-rights/?sh=5c39f0691cfe.

12. Myrna Blyth, *Spin Sisters* (New York: St. Martin's Press, 2004).

13. Meredith Clark, "Ketanji Brown Jackson Photographed by Annie Leibovitz for Vogue," Yahoo! News, August 16, 2022, https://www.yahoo.com/news /ketanji-brown-jackson-photographed-annie-214452918.html?guccounter=1.

14. Kelly Lester, live presentation, Virginia, August 13, 2022; Kelly Lester and Dave Franco, "Abortion Industry Quitter of the Month: Kelly," And Then There Were None, https://abortionworker.com/abortion-industry-quitter-of -the-month-kelly/.

15. Takisha with Dave Franco, "Abortion Industry Quitter of the Month: Takisha," And Then There Were None, https://abortionworker.com/abortion -industry-quitter-of-the-month-takisha.

16. U.S. Department of Homeland Security Center for Countering Human Trafficking, *Countering Human Trafficking: Year in Review* (Washington, D.C.: U.S. Department of Homeland Security, 2022).

17. Kathleen Wilson, private conversation with the author, October 7, 2022.

18. Ibid.

19. Ibid.

20. Thomas Sowell, *The Vision of the Anointed: Self-Congratulation as a Basis for Social Policy* (New York: BasicBooks, 1995), 136.

21. Students for Life, "The Future Is Anti-Abortion—Kristan Hawkins University of Texas San Antonio," YouTube, April 13, 2022, starting at 48:00, https://www.youtube.com/watch?v=REsqZpJO3gs.

22. For the *TIME* magazine cover, see "Kate Millett | Aug. 31, 1970," *TIME*, https://content.time.com/time/covers/0,16641,19700831,00.html; for the cover story, see "Who's Come a Long Way, Baby?," *TIME*, August 31, 1970, https://content.time.com/time/subscriber/article/0,33009,876783,00.html.

23. Khazan, "Why Do Women Bully."

24. Charlotte Gordon, *Romantic Outlaws*: *The Extraordinary Lives of Mary Wollstonecraft and Her Daughter Mary Shelley* (New York: Random House, 2015), 544.

25. Ibid., 477.

26. Emma Specter, "The 9 Funniest Female Comedians of All Time," *Vogue*, March 16, 2022, https://www.vogue.com/article/funniest-female-comedians.

27. "Planned Parenthood's Top Doctor, Praised by CEO, Uses Partial-Birth Abortions to Sell Baby Parts," The Center for Medical Progress, July 14, 2015, https://www.centerformedicalprogress.org/2015/07/planned-parenthoods-top-doctor-praised-by-ceo-uses-partial-birth-abortions-to-sell-baby-parts/.

28. Dave Andrusko, "Abortion Is the Leading Cause of Death Worldwide for the Fourth Year in a Row: 44 Million Lost Lives," Pregnancy Help News, January 9, 2023, https://pregnancyhelpnews.com/abortion-is-the-leading-cause-of-death-worldwide-for-the-fourth-year-in-a-row-44-million-lost-lives; "Abortions This Year," Worldometer, December 31, 2022, available through the Internet Archive, http://web.archive.org/web/20221231234927/https:/www.worldometers.info/.

29. "Documenting Numbers of Victims of the Holocaust and Nazi Persecution," United States Holocaust Memorial Museum, December 8, 2020, https://encyclopedia.ushmm.org/content/en/article/documenting-numbers-of-victims-of-the-holocaust-and-nazi-persecution; Bill Keller, "Major Soviet Paper Says 20 Million Died as Victims of Stalin," *New York Times*, February 4, 1989, https://www.nytimes.com/1989/02/04/world/major-soviet-paper-says-20-million-died-as-victims-of-stalin.html.

Chapter 8: Patriarchy Smashing

1. "The Gospel of Discontent," *Lucifer*, April 7, 1897.

2. Phyllis Chesler, *A Politically Incorrect Feminist: Creating a Movement with Bitches, Lunatics, Dykes, Prodigies, Warriors, and Wonder Women* (New York: St. Martin's Press, 2018), 49.

3. Ibid.

4. David Schweickart, "On Socialist Envy," *Theoria: A Journal of Social and Political Theory*, no. 83/84 (October 1994): 37.

5. Joyce Benenson with Henry Markovits, *Warriors and Worriers: The Survival of the Sexes* (New York: Oxford University Press, 2014), 130.

6. On Flexner's being a communist, see Ellen Carol DuBois, "Overlooked No More: Eleanor Flexner, Pioneering Feminist in an Anti-Feminist Age," *New York Times*, October 16, 2020, https://www.nytimes.com/2020/10/16/obituaries/eleanor-flexner-overlooked.html.

7. Thomas Sowell, *Economic Facts and Fallacies* (New York: Basic Books, 2008), chapter 3.

8. Chesler, *Politically Incorrect Feminist*, 31.

9. Mary Louise Kelly, Mallory Yu, and Courtney Dorning, "Activist Gloria Steinem Reflects on Abortion Rights as They Hang in the Balance," NPR, December 9, 2021, https://www.npr.org/2021/12/09/1062791724/activist -gloria-steinem-reflects-on-abortion-rights-as-they-hang-in-the-balance.

10. Jordan B Peterson, "Modern Times: Camille Paglia & Jordan B Peterson," YouTube, October 2, 2017, starting at 36:30, https://www.youtube.com/ watch?v=v-hIVnmUdXM.

11. Ibid.

12. Philip Rieff, *Charisma: The Gift of Grace, and How It Has Been Taken Away from Us* (New York: Vintage Books, 2008), 28, 30–31.

13. Gabriel Hays, "Goldberg Dehumanizes Nonviable Unborn Children as 'Toxic Thing' in Mother's Womb, Denies Fetal Heartbeat," Fox News, September 28, 2022, https://www.foxnews.com/media/goldberg -dehumanizes-nonviable-unborn-children-toxic-thing-mothers-womb-denies -fetal-heartbeat.

14. Kat Sark, "Gloria Steinem—Happy 80th Birthday and Thank You!," Suites Culturelles (WordPress), March 28, 2014, https://suitesculturelles.wordpress .com/2014/03/28/gloria-steinem-happy-80th-birthday-and-thank-you/.

15. Houston Keene and Jessica Chasmar, "Elizabeth Warren Accused Pro-Life Pregnancy Centers of 'Torturing' Women. Here's What They Actually Do," Fox News, July 26, 2022, https://www.foxnews.com/politics/elizabeth -warren-accused-pro-life-pregnancy-centers-torturing-women.

16. Margaret Thatcher, "Speech to Conservative Party Conference," Margaret Thatcher Foundation, October 10, 1975, https://www.margaretthatcher.org /document/102777.

17. Louise Perry, *The Case against the Sexual Revolution: A New Guide to Sex in the 21st Century* (Cambridge: Polity Press, 2022), 243.

18. Ibid.

Part III: No Girls

1. Mary Livermore, writer and early suffragette, "Suffragists Organize: American Woman Suffrage Organization," National Women's History Museum, 2015, http://www.crusadeforthevote.org/awsa-organize.

2. Elizabeth Hawes, *Why Women Cry, or Wenches with Wrenches* (New York: Reynal and Hitchcock, Inc., 1943), 221.

3. Betty Friedan, "Sex, Society, and the Female Dilemma: A Dialogue between Simone de Beauvoir and Betty Friedan," *Saturday Review*, June 14, 1975.

4. Marie Shear, "Media Watch: Celebrating Women's Words," *New Directions for Women* 15, no. 3 (May/June 1986): 6. Apparently, this quote is frequently incorrectly attributed to Cheris Kramarae and Paula Treichler and their book, *A Feminist Dictionary*.

5. Betty Stoneman, "Radicalesbians and Nietzsche: Slave Morality and the Uberfrau," For the Love of Wisdom (WordPress), December 29, 2013, https://bettystoneman.wordpress.com/2013/12/29/radicalesbians-and -nietzsche-slave-morality-and-the-uberfrau/. A similar articulation can be found here: "Radicalesbians, the Woman Identified Woman," WGS10016, 2022, https://web.archive.org/web/20220626171316/https://wgs10016 .commons.gc.cuny.edu/radicalesbians-the-woman-identified-woman/.

Chapter 9: Margaret and Ls

1. "A Timeline of Lesbian, Gay, Bisexual, and Transgender History in the United States," GSAFE, https://www.gsafewi.org/wp-content/uploads/ US-LGBT-Timeline-UPDATED.pdf.

2. Lillian Faderman, *The Gay Revolution: The Story of Struggle* (New York: Simon & Schuster, 2015), 57.

3. Ibid., 158.

4. Stephen G. Adubato, "Camille Paglia's Second Wave," *American Conservative*, August 5, 2022, https://www.theamericanconservative.com/ camille-paglias-second-wave/.

5. George Luke, "John Money, David Reimer, and the Dark Origins of the Trans Movement," Intellectual Takeout, November 5, 2019, https:// intellectualtakeout.org/2019/11/john-money-david-reimer-and-the-dark -origins-of-the-transgender-movement/. See also Jennifer Roback Morse, *The Sexual State* (Gastonia, North Carolina: TAN Books, 2018).

6. Alfred C. Kinsey, Wardell B. Pomeroy, and Clyde E. Martin, *Sexual Behavior in the Human Male* (Philadelphia: W. B. Saunders Co., 1948; Bloomington, Indiana: Indiana University Press, 1975), 178–80.

7. Faderman, *Gay Revolution*, 174. "The *Berkeley Barb*'s comment on the woman's participation was, 'Ironically, it was a chick who gave the rallying cry to fight.'" Leo E. Laurence, "Gays Hit New York Cops," *Berkeley Barb*, July 4–10, 1969, quoted in Faderman, *Gay Revolution*, 680n14.

8. Faderman, *Gay Revolution*, 174.

9. Ibid., 181–82.

10. Alix Dobkin, interview with Laurel Galana and Gina Covina, in *The New Lesbians: Interviews with Women across the U.S. and Canada* (Berkeley,

California: Moon Books, 1977), 41, quoted in Faderman, *Gay Revolution*, 240.

11. Martha Shelley, "Stepin Fetchit Woman," *Come Out!*, November 1969.

12. Faderman, *Gay Revolution*, 240.

13. Kate Millett, *Flying* (Chicago: University of Illinois Press, 2000), 15.

14. Phyllis Chesler, *A Politically Incorrect Feminist: Creating a Movement with Bitches, Lunatics, Dykes, Prodigies, Warriors, and Wonder Women* (New York: St. Martin's Press, 2018), 242; Mad Dyke, "Angela Davis Is a Dyke and Don't You Forget It," Medium, June 29, 2020, https://medium.com/mad-dyke/angela-davis-is-a-dyke-and-dont-you-forget-it-a71c45c054d5; Ariel Levy, "The Prisoner of Sex," *New York*, May 27, 2005, https://nymag.com/nymetro/news/people/features/11907/; Blanche Linden-Ward and Celeste Deroche, "Robin Morgan," in *American Women Writers: A Critical Reference Guide from Colonial Times to the Present*, Encyclopedia.com, https://www.encyclopedia.com/arts/news-wires-white-papers-and-books/morgan-robin.

15. Bonnie J. Morris, "A Brief History of Lesbian, Gay, Bisexual, and Transgender Social Movements," American Psychological Association, July 21, 2017, https://www.apa.org/pi/lgbt/resources/history.

16. Faderman, *Gay Revolution*, 218.

17. NCBUniversal Archives, "Anita Bryant's Pie to the Face—www.NBCUniversalArchives.com," YouTube, June 9, 2014, https://www.youtube.com/watch?v=5tHGmSh7f-0.

18. Katy Steinmetz, "See Obama's 20-Year Evolution on LGBT Rights," *TIME*, April 10, 2015, https://time.com/3816952/obama-gay-lesbian-transgender-lgbt-rights/.

19. Margaret Sanger, *An Autobiography* (New York: W. W. Norton & Company, 1938), 61.

20. "Margaret Sanger (1879–1966)," PBS, https://www.pbs.org/wgbh/americanexperience/features/pill-margaret-sanger-1879-1966/.

21. Margaret Sanger, *Woman and the New Race* (New York: Brentanos Publishers, 1920), 4.

22. See Angela Franks, *Margaret Sanger's Eugenic Legacy: The Control of Female Fertility* (Jefferson, North Carolina: McFarland & Company, Inc., Publishers, 2005).

23. Ibid., 7.

24. Sanger, *Woman and the New Race*, 5.

25. Ibid., 53.

26. Sanger, *Autobiography*, 109.

27. Ibid., 109–10.

28. Wilhelm Reich, *The Sexual Revolution: Toward a Self-Regulating Character Structure*, trans. Therese Pol (New York: Ferrar, Straus, and Giroux, 1974), chapter 1.

29. Carl R. Trueman, *The Rise and Triumph of the Modern Self: Cultural Amnesia, Expressive Individualism, and the Road to Sexual Revolution* (Wheaton: Crossway, 2020), 237.

30. Ibid., 262.

31. Kate Millett, preface to the Touchstone Paperback, 1990, in Millett, *Flying*.

Chapter 10: Simone and T

1. Allison P. Davis, "Meghan of Montecito," The Cut, August 29, 2022, https://www.thecut.com/article/meghan-markle-profile-interview.html.

2. Sartre and de Beauvoir's existentialism was built upon Friedrich Nietzsche's radical notion of self-creation, especially in the idea of the Superman.

3. Debra Bergoffen and Megan Burke, "Simone de Beauvoir," in *The Stanford Encyclopedia of Philosophy*, ed. Edward N. Zalta (Winter 2021 edition), https://web.archive.org/web/20220114162835/https://plato.stanford.edu/entries/beauvoir/.

4. Simone de Beauvoir, *The Second Sex* (New York Vintage Books, 2010), 283, Kindle.

5. Ibid.

6. Judith Butler, *Gender Trouble: Feminism and the Subversion of Identity* (New York: Routledge, 1990), 12.

7. Abigail Shrier, *Irreversible Damage* (Washington, D.C.: Regnery Publishing, 2020), 7.

8. Ibid., 7–8.

9. Ibid., 4.

10. Ibid.

11. Cecilia Dhejne et al., "Long-Term Follow-Up of Transsexual Persons Undergoing Sex Reassignment Surgery: Cohort Study in Sweden," *PLOS ONE* 6, no. 2 (2011): e16885, https://journals.plos.org/plosone/article?id=10.1371/journal.pone.0016885.

12. "Masculinizing Hormone Therapy," Cleveland Clinic, last reviewed February 3, 2022, https://my.clevelandclinic.org/health/treatments/22322-masculinizing-hormone-therapy; Giuseppe Loverro et al., "Uterine and Ovarian Changes during Testosterone Administration in Young Female-to-Male Transsexuals," *Taiwan Journal of Obstetrics and Gynecology* 55, no. 5 (October 2016): 686–91, https://pubmed.ncbi.nlm.nih.gov/27751416/; Maddie Deutsch, "Information on Testosterone Hormone Therapy," UCSF

Transgender Care, July 2020, https://transcare.ucsf.edu/article/information
-testosterone-hormone-therapy.

13. Andy Rose, "Vanderbilt Transgender Health Clinic Suspends Gender-
Affirming Surgeries for Minors," CNN, October 9, 2022, https://www.cnn
.com/2022/10/09/us/vanderbilt-suspends-gender-affirming-surgery-minors;
Amanda Prestigiacomo, "'Huge Money Maker': Video Reveals Vanderbilt's
Shocking Gender 'Care,' Threats against Dissenting Doctors," Daily Wire+,
September 20, 2022, https://www.dailywire.com/news/huge-money-maker
-video-reveals-vanderbilts-shocking-gender-care-threats-against-dissenting
-doctors.

14. See, e.g., "What Do I Need to Know about Trans and Nonbinary Health
Care?," Planned Parenthood, 2023, https://www.plannedparenthood.org
/learn/gender-identity/transgender/what-do-i-need-know-about-trans-health
-care.

15. Elizabeth R. Sowell et al., "*In Vivo* Evidence for Post-Adolescent Brain
Maturation in Frontal and Striatal Regions," *Nature Neuroscience* 2, no. 10
(1999): 859–61.

16. Vicki Thorn, private conversation with the author, September 17, 2015.

17. Anonymous, "Transgender's Connection with Pornography: It's
Undeniable," Parents with Inconvenient Truths about Trans (PITT)
(Substack), October 11, 2021, https://pitt.substack.com/p/transgenders
-connection-with-pornography.

18. Chloe Cole, who was hastily transitioned as a young teen, became depressed
after her double mastectomy. "She said she felt 'like a monster.'" Mark Judge,
"The Bravery and Brilliance of Detransitioner Chloe Cole," The Stream,
January 11, 2023, https://stream.org/the-bravery-and-brilliance-of
-detransitioner-chloe-cole/.

19. Herbert Marcuse, *One Dimensional Man: Studies in the Ideology of
Advanced Industrial Society* (Boston: Beacon Press, 1964), 9.

Part IV: The Way Home

1. Philip Rieff, *The Triumph of the Therapeutic: Uses of Faith after Freud*, 40th
anniversary ed. (Wilmington, Delaware: Intercollegiate Studies Institute,
2006), 4.

2. Ibid., 10.

3. Ibid., 4.

Chapter 11: Restoration

1. Louise Perry, *The Case against the Sexual Revolution: A New Guide to Sex in the 21st Century* (Cambridge: Polity Press, 2022), 243.
2. J. D. Unwin, *Sex and Culture* (London: Oxford University Press, 1934), 412.
3. Ibid., 412.
4. Ibid., 431.
5. Ibid., 413–14.
6. Ibid., 317.
7. J. D. Unwin, *Hopousia, or The Sexual and Economic Foundations of a New Society* (London: George Allen and Unwin LTD, 1940), 84–85.
8. Unwin, *Sex and Culture*, 420.
9. New World Encyclopedia, s.v. "Arnold J. Toynbee," https://www. newworldencyclopedia.org/entry/Arnold_J._Toynbee.
10. Whittaker Chambers, *Witness*, 50th anniversary ed. (Washington, D.C.: Regnery Gateway, 1980), 8.
11. Ibid., 9.
12. Mary A. Nicholas and Paul Kengor, *The Devil and Bella Dodd: One Woman's Struggle against Communism and Her Redemption* (Gastonia: TAN Books, 2022), 158.
13. Philip Rieff, *My Life among Deathworks: Illustrations of the Aesthetics of Authority*, ed. Kenneth S. Piver, vol. 1, *Sacred Order/Social Order* (Charlottesville, Virginia: University of Virginia Press, 2006), chapter 1.
14. Philip Rieff, *The Triumph of the Therapeutic: Uses of Faith after Freud*, (Wilmington, Delaware: ISI Books, 2006), 19.
15. Rieff, *My Life among Deathworks*, 24.
16. Ibid., 26.
17. Ibid.
18. Ibid., 18.
19. Rieff, *Triumph of the Therapeutic*, 14.

Chapter 12: Mother

1. Gloria Steinem, *My Life on the Road* (New York: Random House, 2015), 230, Kindle.
2. Max Scheler, *Ressentiment*, trans. Louis A. Coser (1915; Milwaukee: Marquette University Press, 1994), 32.
3. vyvansemmomy (@boopyshmurda), "self-reflection on hookup culture," TikTok, September 8, 2021, 4:54 p.m., https://www.tiktok.com/@ vyvansemommy/video/7005669146797100294.

4. Louise Perry, *The Case against the Sexual Revolution: A New Guide to Sex in the 21st Century* (Cambridge: Polity Press, 2022), 254.
5. vyvansemmomy (@boopyshmurda), "self-reflection on hookup culture."
6. Perry, *Case against the Sexual Revolution*, 254
7. For further reading see Erich Neumann, *The Great Mother: An Analysis of the Archetype* (Princeton, New Jersey: Princeton University Press, 2015).
8. Edith Stein, *Essay on Woman* (Washington, D.C.: ICS Publications, 1996), 132.
9. Brittany Wong, "More Women Are Saying No to Motherhood: Will Society Ever Listen?," HuffPost, July 9, 2021, https://www.huffpost.com/entry/child -free-by-choice-women_l_60b7e5c5e4b001ebd46d5601.
10. Judith Wellman, *The Road to Seneca Fall: Elizabeth Cady Stanton and the First Woman's Rights Convention* (Urbana and Chicago: University of Illinois Press, 2004), 10.
11. Mallory Millett, private conversation with the author, October 13, 2022.

Acknowledgments

1. Carrie Gress, "Are Pro-Aborts Burning through Their Credibility?," *Epoch Times*, June 29, 2022, https://www.theepochtimes.com/are-pro-aborts-burning-through-their-credibility_4563450.html.

    Carrie Gress, "The Fashion of Abortion," *Catholic World Report*, October 2, 2015, https://www.catholicworldreport.com/2015/10/02/the-fashion-of-abortion.

    Carrie Gress, "Hollywood's Abortion Obsession Is Based on 1970s Science and Harvey Weinstein Morality," *Washington Examiner*, June 25, 2019, https://www.washingtonexaminer.com/opinion/op-eds/hollywoods-abortion-obsession-is-based-on-1970s-science-and-harvey-weinstein-morality.

    Carrie Gress, "The Little Sisters of the Poor v. The Big Sisters of the Rich," *Catholic World Report*, July 16, 2015, https://www.catholicworldreport.com/2015/07/16/the-little-sisters-of-the-poor-v-the-big-sisters-of-the-rich.

    Carrie Gress, "Second-Wave Feminists Pushed the Sexual Revolution to End America, and It's Working," The Federalist, April 19, 2022, https://thefederalist.com/2022/04/19/second-wave-feminists-pushed-the-sexual -revolution-to-end-america-and-its-working.

    Carrie Gress, "Time for a Restoration—of Women's Glory," The Catholic Thing, https://www.thecatholicthing.org/2021/03/09/time-for -a-restoration-of-womens-glory.

    Carries Gress, "Today's Slave Traders Get Botox," The Stream, May 23, 2021, https://stream.org/todays-slave-traders-get-botox/.

Carries Gress, "Why Don't We Tell Women What's Making Them Miserable?," *National Review*, August 29, 2021, https://www.nationalreview.com/2021/08/why-dont-we-tell-women-whats-making-them-miserable.

Carries Gress, "Why the Cultural Assault on Natural Womanhood Robs Women of Fulfillment," The Federalist, April 26, 2021, https://thefederalist.com/2021/04/26/the-assault-on-the-natural-biological-facets-of-womanhood-robs-women-of-fulfillment.

Carrie Gress, "The War against Our Lady and Womanhood Marches On," *National Catholic Register*, July 23, 2021, https://www.ncregister.com/commentaries/the-war-against-our-lady-and-womanhood-marches-on.

Index